Better Homes and Gardens®

CHRISTMAS COOKING
FROM THE HEART™

Joyful Memories

Meredith® Consumer Marketing
Des Moines, Iowa

CHRISTMAS COOKING
FROM THE HEART™

MEREDITH CORPORATION CONSUMER MARKETING
Vice President, Consumer Marketing: Janet Donnelly
Consumer Marketing Product Director: Heather Sorensen
Consumer Marketing Product Manager: Janece Schwartzkopf
Business Director: Ron Clingman
Senior Production Manager: Al Rodruck
Photographers: Karla Conrad, Jason Donnelly

WATERBURY PUBLICATIONS, INC.
Editorial Director: Lisa Kingsley
Creative Director: Ken Carlson
Associate Editors: Tricia Bergman, Mary Williams
Associate Design Director: Doug Samuelson
Graphic Designer: Mindy Samuelson
Contributing Copy Editor: Terri Fredrickson
Contributing Proofreader: Peg Smith
Contributing Indexer: Elizabeth T. Parson
Contributing Food Stylists: Sue Hoss, Annie Peterson
Contributing Prop Stylist: Lori Hellander

BETTER HOMES AND GARDENS® MAGAZINE
Editor in Chief: Gayle Goodson Butler
Art Director: Michael D. Belknap
Senior Deputy Editor: Nancy Wall Hopkins
Editorial Assistant: Renee Irey

MEREDITH PUBLISHING GROUP
President: Tom Harty

MEREDITH CORPORATION
Chairman and Chief Executive Officer: Stephen M. Lacy

In Memoriam: E.T. Meredith III (1933–2003)

Our seal assures you that every recipe in *Christmas Cooking from the Heart*™ has been tested in the Better Homes and Gardens® Test Kitchen. This means that each recipe is practical and reliable and it meets our high standards of taste appeal. We guarantee your satisfaction with this book for as long as you own it.

All of us at Meredith® Consumer Marketing are dedicated to providing you with information and ideas to enhance your home. We welcome your comments and suggestions. Write to us at: Meredith Consumer Marketing, 1716 Locust St., Des Moines, IA 50309-3023. *Christmas Cooking from the Heart*™ is available by mail. To order editions from past years, call 800/627-5490.

Cover Photography: Jason Donnelly
Front cover: Almond Brickle Ring Cake (page 77)

CINNAMON ROLL
CHRISTMAS
TREE, PAGE 67

PAELLA-STYLE
STUFFING, PAGE 145

Table of Contents

Joyful Memories

CHRISTMAS IS A TIME FOR remembering celebrations of the past as well as making new memories. Some of the best times are shared around the table, surrounded by family and friends. Whether it's a bite of your grandmother's famous German chocolate cake—the one everyone looked forward to all year—or a wonderful new recipe that is destined to become part of future celebrations, food plays a large and tantalizing role in embracing the season. That's what *Better Homes and Gardens Christmas Cooking from the Heart* is all about—giving you recipes and ideas for creating joyful memories this Christmas and for holidays years from now. For a big family feast, look at Oven-Roasted Beef Tenderloin (page 10) or Classic Roast Turkey (page 12). For a celebratory holiday brunch, try Bacon-and-Egg Muffins (page 46) or Pecan-Browned Butter Coffee Cake (page 54). And, of course, there are cookies—from Peppered Orange-Gingerbread Cutouts (page 101) to Peppermint Palmiers(page 95). Happy Memory-Making—and Happy Holidays!

Sharing Traditions

SOME OF THE HAPPIEST HOLIDAY moments happen around the table. Follow these recipes to serve a fabulous holiday feast—from impressive entrees to stuffings, salads, vegetable dishes, soups, and breads.

CLASSIC ROAST
TURKEY, PAGE 12

Oven-Roasted Beef Tenderloin

PREP 30 minutes
ROAST 35 minutes at 425°F
STAND 15 minutes
MAKES 12 servings

1 recipe Peppercorn-Horseradish Sauce
1 tablespoon olive oil
1 3-pound beef tenderloin roast, trimmed
1½ teaspoons kosher salt
1 teaspoon black pepper
Fresh parsley sprigs (optional)

1. Prepare the Peppercorn-Horseradish Sauce. Preheat oven to 425°F. Brush olive oil over meat. For rub, in a small bowl stir together salt and pepper. Sprinkle mixture evenly over meat; rub in with your fingers.
2. Place roast on a rack set in a shallow roasting pan. Insert an oven-going meat thermometer into center of roast. Roast, uncovered, for 35 to 40 minutes or until meat thermometer registers 135°F for medium-rare. (For medium, roast for 45 to 50 minutes or until meat thermometer registers 150°F.)
3. Transfer meat to a cutting board. Cover roast with foil; let stand for 15 minutes. Temperature after standing should be 145°F to 160°F.
4. Slice meat across the grain and arrange on a serving platter. Serve with Peppercorn-Horseradish sauce. If desired, garnish with parsley sprigs.
Peppercorn-Horseradish Sauce In a small bowl stir together 8 ounces sour cream, 3 tablespoons prepared horseradish, 1 tablespoon snipped fresh chives, 2 teaspoons white wine vinegar, and 1 teaspoon coarsely ground black peppercorns. Cover and chill at least 1 hour before serving.
PER SERVING *261 cal., 19 g fat (7 g sat. fat), 91 mg chol., 293 mg sodium, 0 g carb., 0 g fiber, 22 g pro.*

OVEN-ROASTED
BEEF TENDERLOIN

Holiday Ham

PREP 15 minutes
ROAST 1 hour 35 minutes at 325°F
MAKES 20 servings

1 6- to 8-pound cooked ham, rump half
1 cup apricot preserves
1 tablespoon rice vinegar
1 tablespoon Chinese-style hot mustard
1 teaspoon grated fresh ginger or ½ teaspoon ground ginger

1. Preheat oven to 325°F. Score ham by making shallow diagonal cuts in a diamond pattern at 1-inch intervals. Place ham on a rack in a shallow roasting pan. Insert an oven-going thermometer into center of ham (thermometer should not touch bone). Cover with foil. Roast for 1¼ hours.
2. Meanwhile, for the apricot-mustard glaze, in a small bowl stir together the preserves, vinegar, mustard, and ginger.
3. Uncover; roast for 20 to 60 minutes more or until thermometer registers 140°F. Brush ham with some of the glaze during the last 20 minutes of roasting. Serve with remaining glaze.
PER SERVING *241 cal., 13 g fat (4 g sat. fat), 83 mg chol., 1,110 mg sodium, 1 g carb., 0 g fiber, 29 g pro.*

HOLIDAY HAM

Classic Roast Turkey

PREP 15 minutes
ROAST 2 hours 45 minutes at 325°F
STAND 15 minutes
MAKES 10 servings

1 10- to 12-pound turkey
1 recipe Orange and Herb Butter
   Rub and Glaze
   Salt and black pepper
1 recipe Turkey Aromatics
   Vegetable oil

CLASSIC ROAST TURKEY

1. Preheat oven to 325°F. Remove neck and giblets from turkey; discard. Rinse the turkey body cavity; pat dry with paper towels. Use Orange and Herb Butter Rub and Glaze as directed and sprinkle cavity with salt and pepper. Place Turkey Aromatics loosely into cavity. Skewer neck skin to back. Tuck drumstick ends under band of skin across the tail (if present) or tie drumsticks securely to the tail using 100% cotton kitchen string. Twist wing tips under back.

2. Place turkey, breast side up, on a rack in a shallow roasting pan. Brush with oil; sprinkle with additional salt and pepper. Insert an oven-going meat thermometer into the center of an inside thigh muscle (the thermometer should not touch bone). Cover turkey loosely with foil.

3. Roast turkey for 2¼ hours. Remove foil; cut band of skin or string between drumsticks so thighs cook evenly. Roast for 30 to 45 minutes more or until the meat thermometer registers 175°F. (The juices should run clear and drumsticks should move easily in their sockets.) During the last 15 minutes of roasting, brush turkey twice with glaze. Remove turkey from oven. Cover with foil; let stand for 15 to 20 minutes before carving. Transfer turkey to a cutting board to carve. Serve with Perfect Turkey Gravy (right).

Orange and Herb Butter Rub and Glaze In a medium bowl combine ½ cup butter, 2 teaspoons snipped fresh sage, 2 teaspoons snipped fresh rosemary, 2 teaspoons snipped fresh thyme, 1 teaspoon finely shredded orange peel, ½ teaspoon kosher salt, and ¼ teaspoon black pepper. Divide mixture in half. Once the turkey has been rinsed and dried with paper towels, insert your fingers between the skin and meat on the breast to loosen skin. Lift skin and spread half the butter mixture under the skin from front to back of turkey. Continue preparing turkey as directed in Step 1. Place the remaining butter mixture in a microwave-safe bowl; cover. Microwave on high until melted. Stir ⅓ cup honey into butter mixture. Set aside to baste turkey during the last 15 minutes of roasting.

Turkey Aromatics Once the cavity has been sprinkled with salt and pepper, insert 1 medium orange cut into wedges (leave peel on); 1 medium apple cored and cut into wedges; 1 medium onion cut into wedges; 1 small bulb garlic, top and bottom cut off to expose cloves; and 3 sprigs fresh sage, thyme, and/or rosemary into the cavity. Continue preparing turkey as directed in Step 1.

PER SERVING 297 cal., 5 g fat (1 g sat. fat), 179 mg chol., 237 mg sodium, 0 g carb., 0 g fiber, 61 g pro.

Perfect Turkey Gravy

START TO FINISH 15 minutes
MAKES 8 servings

    Reduced-sodium chicken broth
    Pan drippings from roasted
    turkey
    Melted butter (optional)
¼ cup all-purpose flour
    Salt and black pepper

1. Stir 1 cup chicken broth into pan drippings from roasted turkey in roasting pan, scraping up any browned bits from bottom of pan. Pour drippings into a 2-cup glass measuring cup. Skim and reserve fat from drippings. If necessary, add enough melted butter to the reserved fat to equal ¼ cup. Add enough additional broth to the drippings in the measuring cup to equal 2 cups total liquid.

2. Pour the ¼ cup fat into a medium saucepan (discard any remaining fat). Stir in flour.

3. Add broth mixture all at once to saucepan, stirring until smooth. Cook and stir over medium heat until thickened and bubbly. Cook and stir for 1 minute more. Season to taste with salt and pepper.

4. To serve, strain gravy into a serving bowl.

PER SERVING 76 cal., 6 g fat (2 g sat. fat), 7 mg chol., 211 mg sodium, 3 g carb., 0 g fiber, 1 g pro.

Bacon and Mushroom Gravy Prepare gravy as directed. In a large skillet cook 4 strips applewood-smoked bacon until crisp. Transfer bacon to paper towels to drain, reserving drippings in skillet. Add 2 cups sliced fresh cremini and/or button mushrooms to skillet. Cook and stir until mushrooms begin to brown. Crumble bacon. After straining gravy, stir in mushrooms and bacon.

Creamy Mustard and Peppercorn Gravy Prepare gravy as directed, except before adding flour to the fat in Step 2, add ¼ cup chopped shallots (2 medium) and 2 cloves garlic, minced, to the fat; cook and stir over medium heat about 2 minutes or until shallots are tender. Add flour as directed. Stir in ¼ cup whipping cream and 2 teaspoons Dijon mustard with the broth mixture in Step 2. Continue as directed. Stir in 1 teaspoon cracked black pepper. Do not strain gravy.

No-Drippings Gravy Prepare gravy as directed, except replace the fat with ¼ cup butter and replace drippings with reduced-sodium chicken broth or chicken stock.

Focaccia-Artichoke Dressing

PREP 20 minutes
BAKE 40 minutes at 350°F
MAKES 12 servings

- 8 ounces bulk Italian sausage, crumbled
- ¾ cup coarsely chopped red and/or green sweet pepper (1 medium)
- ½ cup coarsely chopped onion (1 medium)
- 3 cloves garlic, minced
- 1 13.75- to 14-ounce can quartered artichoke hearts, drained
- 12 cups dried garlic focaccia cubes*
- ¾ cup finely shredded Parmigiano Reggiano cheese (3 ounces)
- ¼ cup snipped fresh basil
- ¼ cup snipped fresh flat-leaf parsley
- 1¾ to 2¼ cups chicken broth

1. Preheat oven to 350°F. In a large skillet cook sausage, sweet pepper, onion, and garlic over medium-high heat until sausage is cooked and vegetables are tender. Drain off fat. Stir in artichoke hearts.

2. In an extra-large bowl combine bread cubes, ¼ cup of the cheese, the basil, and parsley. Add sausage mixture, tossing to coat. Drizzle with 1¾ cups broth, tossing to combine. Let stand for 5 minutes. Add up to an additional ½ cup broth, as needed, until moistened.

3. Spoon dressing into a 3-quart rectangular baking dish. Sprinkle with the remaining ½ cup cheese; cover with foil. Bake for 40 to 45 minutes or until heated through.

PER SERVING 217 cal., 10 g fat (4 g sat. fat), 20 mg chol., 721 mg sodium, 24 g carb., 2 g fiber, 10 g pro.

*Tip To make dry bread cubes, preheat oven to 300°F. Cut focaccia into ¾-inch cubes (should yield 12 cups). Spread in two 15×10×1-inch baking pans. Bake for 10 to 15 minutes or until dry, stirring twice; cool. (Cubes will continue to dry and crisp as they cool.) Or let bread cubes stand, loosely covered, at room temperature for 8 to 12 hours.

FOCACCIA-ARTICHOKE DRESSING

PUMPERNICKEL
CHERRY STUFFING

Pumpernickel Cherry Stuffing

PREP 20 minutes
BAKE 10 minutes at 350°F
SLOW COOK 4 hours (low) or
2½ hours (high)
MAKES 18 servings

6 cups ¾-inch pumpernickel bread
   cubes
6 cups ¾-inch rye bread cubes
   Nonstick cooking spray
¼ cup butter
2 cups chopped onions (2 large)
1 cup chopped celery (2 stalks)
3 cloves garlic, minced
2 eggs, lightly beaten
1 14.5-ounce can chicken broth

2 cups dried cherries
1 cup chopped pear (1 medium)
1 cup chopped Granny Smith
   apple
¼ cup snipped fresh flat-leaf
   parsley
1 tablespoon snipped fresh sage
½ teaspoon black pepper

1. Preheat oven to 350°F. Spread pumpernickel and rye bread cubes in two 15×10×1-inch baking pans. Bake for 10 to 15 minutes or until bread is dry and lightly toasted, stirring twice; cool.
2. Lightly coat a 5- to 6-quart slow cooker with cooking spray; set aside. In a large skillet melt butter over medium-high heat. Add onions and celery; cook about 5 minutes or until tender, stirring occasionally. Add garlic; cook and stir for 1 minute more.
3. In a large bowl combine eggs and broth. Stir in onion mixture, dried cherries, pear, apple, parsley, sage, and pepper. Fold in bread cubes until moistened. Transfer bread mixture to the prepared cooker.
4. Cover and cook on low-heat setting for 4 to 6 hours or on high-heat setting for 2½ to 3 hours. Serve immediately or keep warm, covered, on warm-heat setting up to 2 hours.
PER SERVING *160 cal., 4 g fat
(2 g sat. fat), 31 mg chol., 292 mg sodium,
30 g carb., 3 g fiber, 4 g pro.*

Olive Relish

PREP 35 minutes CHILL 2 hours
MAKES 2 cups

- 1 cup chopped French green olives with Herbes de Provence, French green Picholine olives, or pimiento-stuffed green olives
- ½ cup pepperoncini, stems removed and chopped
- 1 small carrot, finely chopped
- ¼ cup capers, drained
- ¼ cup roasted red sweet peppers, drained and chopped
- ¼ cup extra virgin olive oil
- 2 tablespoons snipped fresh flat-leaf parsley
- 2 tablespoons red wine vinegar
- 2 tablespoons finely chopped red onion
- 2 cloves garlic, minced

1. In a medium bowl combine olives, pepperoncini, carrot, capers, roasted peppers, oil, parsley, vinegar, onion, and garlic; mix lightly. Cover and chill for 2 to 24 hours.

PER SERVING *87 cal., 9 g fat (0 g sat. fat), 0 mg chol., 667 mg sodium, 2 g carb., 0 g fiber, 0 g pro.*

EASY PARMESAN-
FENNEL ROLLS

Apricot-Date Chutney

PREP 40 minutes COOK 15 minutes
MAKES 16 servings

- 1 tablespoon vegetable oil
- 1 cup chopped onion (1 large)
- 2 teaspoons grated fresh ginger
- 4 cloves garlic, minced
- ⅔ cup sugar
- ½ cup red wine vinegar
- ¼ cup lemon juice
- ½ teaspoon dry mustard
- ½ teaspoon ground allspice
- 3 cups chopped, peeled ripe apricots (8 to 12 medium)
- ¾ cup snipped, pitted dates

1. In a medium-size heavy stainless-steel, enamel, or nonstick saucepan heat oil over medium heat. Add onions, ginger, and garlic. Cook until onion is tender, stirring occasionally. Stir in sugar, vinegar, lemon juice, mustard, and allspice. Bring to boiling, stirring to dissolve sugar; reduce heat. Simmer, uncovered, for 5 minutes.

2. Stir apricots and dates into the onion mixture. Return to boiling; reduce heat. Simmer, uncovered, for about 10 minutes or until chutney is thickened, stirring occasionally. Remove from heat.

3. Serve chutney warm or at room temperature.

PER SERVING *39 cal., 0 g fat, 0 mg chol., 1 mg sodium, 9 g carb., 1 g fiber, 0 g pro.*

Easy Parmesan-Fennel Rolls

PREP 25 minutes RISE 30 minutes
BAKE 10 minutes at 375°F
MAKES 12 servings

- 1 16-ounce loaf frozen white or wheat bread dough
- 1 tablespoon grated Parmesan cheese
- 2 teaspoons yellow cornmeal
- ½ teaspoon fennel seeds
- 2 tablespoons butter, melted

1. Thaw dough according to package directions. Grease a large baking sheet; set aside. In a small bowl stir together Parmesan cheese, cornmeal, and fennel seeds; set aside.

2. Divide dough into 12 pieces. Gently shape each piece into a ball by pulling dough and pinching underneath. Place balls 2 to 3 inches apart on the prepared baking sheet. Using kitchen shears, cut two deep snips to form an "X" in the top of each bun. Cover with waxed paper and let rise in a warm place about 30 minutes or until nearly double in size. Gently brush with melted butter and sprinkle with cheese mixture.

3. Preheat oven to 375°F. Uncover rolls. Bake for 10 to 15 minutes or until golden. Transfer rolls to a wire rack. Cool slightly before serving.

PER SERVING *117 cal., 3 g fat (1 g sat. fat), 5 mg chol., 194 mg sodium, 18 g carb., 0 g fiber, 2 g pro.*

PEPPERED BACON, GREEN ONION, AND BUTTERMILK SCONES

Peppered Bacon, Green Onion, and Buttermilk Scones

PREP 30 minutes
BAKE 15 minutes at 425°F
MAKES 26 servings

- 6 slices peppered bacon
- ½ cup finely chopped green onions (4)
- 1 egg, lightly beaten
- 1 cup buttermilk or sour milk*
- 3 cups all-purpose flour
- 1 tablespoon baking powder
- ¼ teaspoon garlic powder
- ¼ teaspoon cayenne pepper or crushed red pepper
- ½ cup butter
- 1½ cups finely shredded Gruyère cheese (6 ounces)

1. In an extra-large skillet cook bacon over medium heat until crisp. Remove bacon and drain on paper towels, reserving 2 tablespoons drippings in skillet. Crumble bacon; set aside. Add green onions to the reserved drippings. Cook and stir over medium heat until tender. Set aside.
2. Preheat oven to 425°F. Line a large baking sheet with parchment paper. In a bowl combine egg and buttermilk.
3. In a large bowl stir together flour, baking powder, garlic powder, and cayenne pepper. Using a pastry blender, cut in butter until mixture resembles coarse crumbs. Stir in crumbled bacon, green onions, and cheese. Make a well in the center of flour mixture. Reserve 2 tablespoons of the buttermilk mixture. Add the remaining buttermilk mixture all at once to flour mixture. Using a fork, stir just until moistened.
4. Turn dough out onto a lightly floured surface. Knead dough by folding and gently pressing it for 10 to 12 strokes or until nearly smooth. Roll dough to ½ inch thickness. Using a 2- to 2½-inch round cutter, cut out dough. Place dough rounds, nearly touching, on the prepared baking sheet. Brush with the reserved 2 tablespoons buttermilk mixture.
5. Bake for 15 minutes or until golden. Transfer scones to wire racks; cool.
PER SERVING *137 cal., 8 g fat (4 g sat. fat), 27 mg chol., 155 mg sodium, 12 g carb., 0 g fiber, 5 g pro.*
***Tip** To make 1 cup sour milk, place 1 tablespoon lemon juice or vinegar in a glass measuring cup. Add enough milk to equal 1 cup liquid; stir. Let stand for 5 minutes before using.

Roasted Beet and Asiago Risotto

PREP 30 minutes
ROAST 40 minutes at 375°F
COOK 30 minutes
MAKES 6 servings

- 1½ pounds fresh red beets (3 medium)
- 1 tablespoon olive oil
- ¼ teaspoon salt
- ½ teaspoon black pepper
- ⅔ cup chopped onion (1 large)
- 2 tablespoons butter
- 2 cloves garlic, minced
- 1⅓ cups arborio rice
- ¼ cup Prosecco or dry white wine
- 4 cups reduced-sodium chicken broth
- 2 sprigs fresh thyme
- ¼ cup finely shredded Asiago cheese (1 ounce)
  Fresh thyme leaves
  Shaved Asiago cheese

1. Preheat oven to 375°F. Wash and peel beets. Cut each beet into eight wedges. Place in a 13×9×2-inch baking pan. Toss with the olive oil, salt, and ¼ teaspoon of the pepper. Cover the pan tightly with foil. Roast for 20 minutes. Remove foil from pan; stir beets gently. Roast, uncovered, for 20 to 25 minutes more or until tender. Set six wedges aside as garnish.
2. Meanwhile, in a large saucepan cook onion in hot butter until tender. Add garlic; cook and stir for 30 seconds. Add rice; cook and stir for 2 minutes more. Remove from heat. Stir in the Prosecco. Add chicken broth, thyme sprigs, and the remaining ¼ teaspoon pepper. Bring to boiling; reduce heat. Simmer, covered, for 20 minutes (do not lift lid). Remove from heat. Let stand, covered, for 5 minutes. (Rice should be tender and slightly firm and risotto should be creamy.)
3. Remove and discard thyme sprigs. Stir in the 18 beet wedges and the ¼ cup Asiago cheese. Transfer risotto to a serving bowl. Garnish with reserved beet wedges, thyme leaves, and Asiago shavings.
PER SERVING *309 cal., 10 g fat (5 g sat. fat), 20 mg chol., 695 mg sodium, 45 g carb., 4 g fiber, 9 g pro.*

ROASTED BEET
AND ASIAGO
RISOTTO

Butternut Squash-Maple Bacon Casserole

PREP 20 minutes   COOK 25 minutes
BAKE 35 minutes at 350°F
STAND 10 minutes
MAKES 12 servings

    4   pounds butternut squash, peeled
        and chopped (about 10½ cups)
    4   eggs, lightly beaten
    ⅓   cup butter, cut up
    ¼   cup packed brown sugar
    ¼   cup maple syrup
    ¼   cup milk
    8   ounces maple-flavor bacon,
        chopped
    1   medium onion, halved and sliced
    ½   teaspoon ground cinnamon
        Maple syrup

1. In a large Dutch oven cook butternut squash, covered, in enough boiling salted water to cover for 25 to 30 minutes or until tender; drain. Return to pan.

2. Preheat oven to 350°F. Grease a 3-quart baking dish; set aside. Mash squash with a potato masher. Gradually stir about 1 cup of the mashed hot squash into the beaten eggs. Return mixture to remaining squash in pan. Add butter, brown sugar, the ¼ cup maple syrup, and the milk. Stir until well combined. Transfer to the prepared baking dish.

3. Bake, uncovered, for 25 minutes. Meanwhile, in a large skillet cook bacon and onion over medium heat about 10 minutes or until bacon is slightly crispy and onion is tender, stirring frequently. Remove from heat, drain off any excess fat. Stir in cinnamon.

4. Top casserole with the bacon and onion mixture. Bake, uncovered, about 10 minutes more or until edges are set and casserole is heated through. Drizzle with additional maple syrup. Let stand for 10 minutes before serving.

PER SERVING *269 cal., 15 g fat (7 g sat. fat), 94 mg chol., 410 mg sodium, 28 g carb., 3 g fiber, 8 g pro.*

BUTTERNUT
SQUASH-MAPLE
BACON CASSEROLE

Lemon-Garlic Mashed Potatoes

PREP 20 minutes COOK 20 minutes
MAKES 16 servings

- 3 pounds Yukon gold potatoes, scrubbed and cut in chunks
- 4 cloves garlic, halved
- 3 tablespoons olive oil
- 2 tablespoons butter
- ½ teaspoon salt
- ¼ teaspoon black pepper
- 2 tablespoons capers, drained and chopped
- ⅓ cup chopped fresh flat-leaf parsley
- 2 teaspoons finely shredded lemon peel
- 1 lemon half

1. In a large saucepan cook potatoes and garlic in lightly salted boiling water, covered, for 20 to 25 minutes or until tender.

2. Drain potatoes, reserving 1 cup cooking water. Using a potato masher, mash potatoes to desired consistency. Add 2 tablespoons of the olive oil, butter, salt, pepper, and enough of the reserved liquid to reach desired consistency. Stir to combine. Transfer to a serving dish. Top with capers, parsley, and lemon peel. Drizzle with remaining olive oil. Squeeze lemon juice over potatoes before serving.

PER SERVING *98 cal., 4 g fat (1 g sat. fat), 4 mg chol., 130 mg sodium, 15 g carb., 2 g fiber, 2 g pro.*

Caramelized Green Beans

PREP 25 minutes COOK 25 minutes
MAKES 6 servings

- ⅓ cup butter
- 1½ pounds green beans, trimmed
- 1 large sweet onion, halved and thinly sliced
- ¾ teaspoon salt
- ¼ teaspoon black pepper
- 2 tablespoons packed brown sugar
- 2 teaspoons snipped fresh rosemary
- ½ cup chopped pecans, toasted* Snipped fresh rosemary

FRUITED MULTIGRAIN PILAF

1. In a large skillet heat butter over medium-low heat. Add green beans and onion. Sprinkle with salt and pepper.

2. Cook beans and onion, turning often with tongs, for 20 minutes. Add brown sugar and the 2 teaspoons rosemary. Cook 5 to 10 minutes more or until beans and onion are caramelized. If edges brown too quickly reduce heat to low.

3. Stir in pecans just before serving. Sprinkle with fresh rosemary.

PER SERVING *213 cal., 17 g fat (7 g sat. fat), 27 mg chol., 389 mg sodium, 15 g carb., 4 g fiber, 3 g pro.*

Fruited Multigrain Pilaf

PREP 20 minutes
SLOW COOK 6 hours
MAKES 12 servings

- ⅔ cup uncooked wheat berries
- ½ cup uncooked pearled farro or regular barley
- ½ cup uncooked wild rice
- 4 cups chicken or vegetable broth
- 12 ounces sweet potato, peeled and chopped (2⅓ cups)
- ⅔ cup dried cranberries
- ½ cup sliced celery (1 stalk)
- 1 tablespoon butter
- 2 cloves garlic, minced
- ½ teaspoon salt
- ¼ teaspoon black pepper
- 1⅓ cups chopped red cooking apples (such as Rome or Jonathan)
- ½ cup chopped walnuts, toasted*
- ½ cup sliced green onions (4)
- 1 tablespoon snipped fresh thyme

1. Rinse and drain wheat berries, farro, and wild rice. In a 3½- or 4-quart slow cooker stir together wheat berries, farro, wild rice, broth, sweet potato, cranberries, celery, butter, garlic, salt, and pepper.

2. Cover and cook on low-heat setting for 6 to 7 hours or on high-heat setting for 3½ to 4 hours. Stir in apples, walnuts, green onions, and thyme.

PER SERVING *186 cal., 5 g fat (1 g sat. fat), 4 mg chol., 418 mg sodium, 32 g carb., 4 g fiber, 5 g pro.*

***Tip** To toast whole nuts or large pieces, spread them in a shallow pan. Bake in a 350°F oven for 5 to 10 minutes, shaking the pan once or twice. Toast coconut in the same way, watching it closely to avoid burning. Toast finely chopped or ground nuts, cumin seeds, or sesame seeds in a dry skillet over medium heat. Stir often to prevent burning.

CAULIFLOWER
SALAD

Cauliflower Salad

START TO FINISH 50 minutes
MAKES 8 servings

- ¼ cup dried cranberries
- ¼ cup snipped dried apricots
- 1 head cauliflower, cut into florets (8 cups)
- 2 tablespoons butter
- 1 tablespoon olive oil
- 1 medium onion, halved and thinly sliced
- 2 cloves garlic, minced
- 1 5-ounce package fresh baby spinach, chopped
- ½ cup roasted pistachios, chopped
- ½ teaspoon salt
- ½ cup sliced green onions (4)

1. Place the dried cranberries and apricots in a small bowl. Cover with boiling water and let stand for 10 minutes or until plump; drain well. Set aside.
2. Meanwhile, place the cauliflower, in batches, in a food processor. Cover and pulse, four to six times for each batch, until crumbly and cauliflower resembles the texture of couscous.
3. In an extra-large skillet heat 1 tablespoon of the butter and the olive oil over medium-high heat. Add the onion; cook and stir about 3 minutes or until tender and just starting to brown. Add garlic; cook and stir for 30 seconds. Add the cauliflower, spreading in an even layer. Cook for 8 minutes or until cauliflower is evenly golden, stirring occasionally. Spread in an even layer.
4. Drain, then stir in the cranberries and apricots, the spinach, pistachios, and salt. Cook and stir until combined.
5. Stir in the remaining 1 tablespoon butter and the green onions. Toss until butter is melted. Transfer to a serving bowl.
PER SERVING *139 cal., 8 g fat (3 g sat. fat), 8 mg chol., 217 mg sodium, 14 g carb., 4 g fiber, 4 g pro.*

Orange- and Balsamic-Glazed Tricolor Carrots

PREP 25 minutes COOK 15 minutes
MAKES 6 servings

- 2 pounds medium-size red, yellow, and/or orange carrots, peeled
- ½ cup orange juice
- ¼ cup balsamic vinegar
- 4 teaspoons sugar
- ¾ teaspoon salt
- ¼ teaspoon black pepper
- 2 tablespoons butter
- 1 tablespoon snipped fresh chives

1. Place a steamer basket in a large saucepan. Add water to just below the bottom of the basket. Bring water to boiling. Add carrots to basket. Cover and reduce heat. Steam for 15 to 20 minutes or just until tender. Transfer carrots to a serving platter; cover and keep warm.
2. Meanwhile, for glaze, in a medium saucepan combine orange juice, balsamic vinegar, sugar, salt, and pepper. Bring to boiling; reduce heat. Simmer, uncovered, about 12 minutes or until reduced to syrup consistency (about ⅓ cup). Stir in butter. Drizzle glaze over carrots and sprinkle with chives.
PER SERVING *126 cal., 4 g fat (2 g sat. fat), 10 mg chol., 432 mg sodium, 21 g carb., 4 g fiber, 2 g pro.*

ORANGE- AND BALSAMIC-GLAZED TRICOLOR CARROTS

BLUE CHEESE BROCCOLI AU GRATIN

5. Bake uncovered for 30 minutes or until bubbly and topping is browned. Let stand for 15 minutes before serving.

PER SERVING *275 cal., 19 g fat (11 g sat. fat), 51 mg chol., 711 mg sodium, 16 g carb., 3 g fiber, 13 g pro.*

Garlicky Crumb-Coated Broccolini

PREP **20 minutes**
COOK **5 minutes**
ROAST **15 minutes at 425°F**
MAKES **8 servings**

- 2 pounds broccolini or broccoli, trimmed
- 1 cup soft bread crumbs
- ¼ cup olive oil
- ¼ cup butter
- 3 tablespoons finely chopped fresh garlic
- ½ cup grated Parmesan cheese
- ⅓ cup chopped pitted green olives
- ⅓ cup finely chopped yellow sweet pepper
- 1 tablespoon finely shredded lemon peel
  Lemon wedges (optional)

1. Preheat oven to 425°F. Arrange broccolini in a shallow roasting pan. Sprinkle with bread crumbs.
2. In a small saucepan combine olive oil, butter, and garlic; heat over low heat, stirring occasionally, until fragrant, about 5 minutes. Drizzle evenly over broccolini. Sprinkle with Parmesan.
3. Roast, uncovered, for 15 to 20 minutes or until broccolini is tender. Transfer to a serving platter or dish. Combine olives, sweet pepper, and lemon peel; sprinkle over broccolini. Pass lemon wedges.

PER SERVING *198 cal., 15 g fat (6 g sat. fat), 20 mg chol., 281 mg sodium, 12 g carb., 4 g fiber, 6 g pro.*

Blue Cheese Broccoli au Gratin

PREP **35 minutes**
BAKE **30 minutes at 375°F**
STAND **15 minutes**
MAKES **10 servings**

- 10 cups broccoli florets (about 2½ pounds)
- 6 tablespoons butter
- ¼ cup all-purpose flour
- 2 cups whole milk
- 1 cup crumbled mild blue cheese (4 ounces)
- 1 cup shredded Gruyère cheese (4 ounces)
- 1 teaspoon salt
- ½ teaspoon black pepper
- 4 slices bacon, crisp-cooked and crumbled
- 1½ cups coarse herbed focaccia bread crumbs
- 2 tablespoons snipped fresh chives

1. Preheat oven to 375°F. Bring a large pot of water to boiling. Add broccoli florets; return to boiling. Cook for 1 minute; drain well. Transfer broccoli to an extra-large bowl.
2. Meanwhile, in a large saucepan melt 4 tablespoons of the butter over medium heat. Add the flour; cook and stir for 2 minutes. Slowly whisk in the milk; cook and stir until sauce comes to boiling. Reduce heat; simmer about 2 minutes or until slightly thickened. Remove from heat; stir in ½ cup of the blue cheese, ½ cup of the Gruyere, ½ teaspoon of the salt, and ¼ teaspoon of the pepper. Pour over the broccoli, tossing to coat.
3. Transfer broccoli mixture to a 3-quart gratin dish or baking dish. Sprinkle with bacon and remaining blue cheese and Gruyère.
4. In a small bowl stir together bread crumbs; the remaining 2 tablespoons butter, melted; the remaining salt and pepper; and the chives. Sprinkle over casserole.

GARLICKY
CRUMB-COATED
BROCCOLINI

Mushroom Fricassée with Fresh Herbs

PREP 25 minutes
COOK 17 minutes
STAND 5 minutes
MAKES 6 servings

2 pounds assorted fresh mushrooms, such as cremini, button, shiitake, chanterelle, porcini, oyster, and/or morels, cleaned and tough stems trimmed
2 tablespoons walnut oil
1 tablespoon butter
½ cup finely chopped shallots (4 medium)
2 cloves garlic, minced
½ teaspoon coarse sea salt
¼ teaspoon black pepper
½ cup Madeira or chicken broth
½ cup whipping cream
1 tablespoon snipped fresh chives
1 to 2 teaspoons snipped fresh rosemary or ¼ to ½ teaspoon dried rosemary, crushed
¼ cup snipped fresh flat-leaf parsley

1. Leave small mushrooms whole, halve medium-size mushrooms, and quarter large mushrooms (12 cups). In an extra-large skillet heat 1 tablespoon of the walnut oil and 1½ teaspoons of the butter over medium heat. Add 6 cups of the mushrooms; cook about 5 minutes or until mushrooms begin to color, stirring occasionally. Using a slotted spoon, transfer mushrooms to a large bowl. Repeat with the remaining mushrooms, oil, and butter. Add the shallots, garlic, and reserved cooked mushrooms to the skillet; cook and stir for 2 to 3 minutes or until the mushrooms are golden and shallots are tender. Stir in salt and pepper.

2. Remove from heat; add the Madeira. Return to heat; simmer about 3 minutes or until the liquid is nearly evaporated. Stir in the cream, chives, and rosemary. Cook about 2 minutes or until cream is slightly thickened. Remove from heat and let stand for 5 minutes. Transfer to a serving bowl and sprinkle with snipped fresh parsley; serve warm.

PER SERVING *193 cal., 14 g fat (6 g sat. fat), 32 mg chol., 231 mg sodium, 9 g carb., 2 g fiber, 6 g pro.*

MUSHROOM FRICASSÉE WITH FRESH HERBS

Brussels Sprouts Casserole with Pancetta and Asiago Cheese

PREP 30 minutes
BAKE 15 minutes at 400°F
MAKES 8 servings

1¼ pounds Brussels sprouts, trimmed and coarsely chopped
1 cup chopped carrots (2 medium)
3 ounces pancetta or 8 slices bacon, chopped
¼ cup finely chopped shallots (2 medium) or ½ cup chopped onion (1 medium)
1 tablespoon butter
3 cloves garlic, minced
1 tablespoon all-purpose flour
1 cup finely shredded Asiago or Parmesan cheese (4 ounces)
½ teaspoon salt
½ teaspoon black pepper
1 cup whipping cream
1 tablespoon coarse ground mustard
Dash crushed red pepper
½ cup panko or other coarse bread crumbs

1. Preheat oven to 400°F. Lightly grease a 1½-quart gratin dish or casserole dish. In a large saucepan cook Brussels sprouts and carrots in lightly salted boiling water for 5 to 6 minutes or until tender; drain well. Return vegetables to saucepan.
2. Meanwhile, in a large skillet cook pancetta over medium heat until crisp. Using a slotted spoon, transfer pancetta to paper towels to drain; reserve drippings in skillet. Add shallots, butter, and garlic to drippings in skillet; cook and stir for 30 seconds. Stir in flour. Stir shallot mixture into saucepan. Stir in pancetta, ½ cup of the cheese, the salt, and black pepper. Spoon into prepared dish.
3. In a small bowl stir together cream, mustard, and crushed red pepper. Pour over vegetables in dish. In another small bowl stir together the remaining ½ cup cheese and the panko. Sprinkle over vegetables.
4. Bake for 15 to 20 minutes or until casserole is bubbly and topping is golden.

PER SERVING 274 cal., 21 g fat (12 g sat. fat), 69 mg chol., 603 mg sodium, 13 g carb., 3 g fiber, 9 g pro.

BRUSSELS SPROUTS CASSEROLE WITH PANCETTA AND ASIAGO CHEESE

ASPARAGUS
WITH
TARRAGON
SAUCE

Asparagus with Tarragon Sauce

START TO FINISH 30 minutes
MAKES 6 servings

1¼ pounds asparagus spears
  2 tablespoons butter
  2 tablespoons finely chopped
    shallot (1 medium)
  2 tablespoons snipped fresh
    tarragon
  ½ teaspoon kosher salt
  ¼ teaspoon cracked black pepper
  ¼ cup mayonnaise
  2 tablespoons Dijon mustard
  2 tablespoons cider vinegar
  1 teaspoon lemon juice
  2 ounces prosciutto, torn or cut
    into 2×1-inch pieces
  2 hard-cooked eggs, coarsely
    chopped
    Snipped fresh tarragon
    Kosher salt and cracked black
    pepper

1. Snap off and discard woody bases
from asparagus. If desired, scrape off
scales.
2. For tarragon sauce, in a small
saucepan melt 1 tablespoon of
the butter over medium heat.
Add shallot; cook and stir about
2 minutes or until softened. Stir in the
2 tablespoons tarragon, ½ teaspoon
salt, and ¼ teaspoon pepper. Stir in
mayonnaise, mustard, vinegar, and
lemon juice. Heat through, stirring
frequently. Cover and keep warm.
3. In a medium skillet heat the
remaining 1 tablespoon butter over
medium-high heat; add prosciutto.
Cook about 2 to 4 minutes or just until
crisp and golden, turning once halfway
through cooking time. Transfer to
paper towels to drain.
4. Bring a large saucepan of salted
water to boiling. Add asparagus and
cook about 3 minutes or until crisp-
tender; drain.
5. Transfer asparagus to a serving
platter. Drizzle with the tarragon
sauce. Sprinkle with prosciutto and
chopped eggs. Sprinkle with additional
snipped fresh tarragon, salt, and
pepper.
PER SERVING 163 cal., 14 g fat
(4 g sat. fat), 86 mg chol., 702 mg sodium,
3 g carb., 1 g fiber, 6 g pro.

Champagne and Poached Pear Salad

PREP 30 minutes
COOK 10 minutes CHILL 2 hours
BAKE 6 minutes at 425°F
MAKES 8 servings

- ¼ cup all-purpose flour
- 1 egg white, lightly beaten
- ¼ cup seasoned fine dry bread crumbs
- 1 8-ounce round Brie or Camembert cheese, cut into 8 wedges
- 1 cup extra-dry champagne, sparkling wine, or apple cider
- ⅓ cup sugar
- ¼ cup water
- ½ teaspoon whole cloves
- ½ teaspoon whole allspice
- 1 inch stick cinnamon
- 1 vanilla bean, halved lengthwise (optional)
- 4 firm, ripe pears, peeled, halved, and cored
- 10 cups mesclun and/or baby spinach
- ⅔ cup dried tart cherries or dried cranberries
- ½ cup broken walnuts or pecans, toasted (see tip, page 19)
- 1 recipe Champagne Vinaigrette

1. For cheese wedges, place flour in a shallow dish. Place egg white in a second shallow dish. In a third shallow dish place bread crumbs. Coat cheese wedges with flour; dip in egg white; dip in bread crumbs to coat. Place coated wedges on a lightly greased baking sheet. Place in freezer.
2. To poach pears, in a large skillet combine champagne, sugar, the water, cloves, allspice, cinnamon, and, if desired, vanilla bean. Bring to boiling over medium heat, stirring to dissolve sugar; reduce heat. Carefully add pear halves to skillet. Cover and simmer for 10 to 12 minutes or just until pears are tender. Remove from heat. Using a slotted spoon, transfer pears to a bowl; discard poaching liquid and spices. Cover pears and refrigerate for 2 hours or until chilled.
3. Preheat oven to 425°F. In a large bowl combine mesclun, half the cherries, and half the toasted walnuts. Pour half the Champagne Vinaigrette over salad; toss lightly to coat. Arrange evenly on salad plates; set aside.
4. Remove cheese from freezer. Bake for 6 to 8 minutes or until cheese is softened, slightly bubbly, and golden brown. If desired, cut pear halves into wedges. Arrange pears and cheese on salad plates. Drizzle with a little more vinaigrette and sprinkle with remaining cherries and walnuts.
Champagne Vinaigrette In a screw-top jar combine ⅓ cup vegetable oil, 3 tablespoons champagne vinegar or white wine vinegar, 1 tablespoon finely chopped shallot, 1 teaspoon honey, ¼ teaspoon salt, and ⅛ teaspoon black pepper. Cover and shake well.

PER SERVING *377 cal., 22 g fat (6 g sat. fat), 28 mg chol., 353 mg sodium, 36 g carb., 6 g fiber, 10 g pro.*

Winter Slaw with Kale and Cabbage

START TO FINISH 25 minutes
MAKES 10 servings

- 4 cups shredded kale, stems removed (4 ounces)
- 1 teaspoon salt
- 1 tablespoon olive oil
- 4 cups shredded savoy cabbage
- 1 cup shredded purple cabbage
- 1 cup shredded carrots (2 medium)
- ¾ cup packed finely snipped flat-leaf parsley
- ⅓ cup mayonnaise
- 3 tablespoons sour cream
- 2 tablespoons sliced green onion (1)
- 1 tablespoon white wine vinegar
- 1 tablespoon snipped fresh tarragon or ¼ teaspoon dried tarragon, crushed
- 1 teaspoon sugar
- 1 clove garlic, minced
- ½ cup pepitas (pumpkin seeds), toasted (see tip, page 19)

1. In an extra-large bowl combine the kale, salt, and olive oil. Using your hands, rub the kale to help soften it and brighten its color. Rinse the kale in a colander under cool running water; drain well and return to the bowl. Add the savoy cabbage, purple cabbage, and carrots; toss to combine. Set slaw aside.
2. For the dressing, in a food processor or blender combine the parsley, mayonnaise, sour cream, green onion, vinegar, tarragon, sugar, and garlic. Cover and process or blend to combine.
3. Add the dressing to the vegetable mixture; toss to coat. Sprinkle pepitas over the salad.

PER SERVING *159 cal., 13 g fat (2 g sat. fat), 5 mg chol., 194 mg sodium, 7 g carb., 3 g fiber, 5 g pro.*

WINTER SLAW WITH KALE AND CABBAGE

MANHATTAN CLAM CHOWDER

Portobello Mushroom and Roasted Garlic Soup

PREP 25 minutes
BAKE 45 minutes at 325°F
COOK 51 minutes   MAKES 6 servings

- 1 whole garlic bulb
- 2 teaspoons olive oil
- 1 pound fresh portobello mushrooms
- 1 cup sliced celery (2 stalks)
- 1 cup chopped red or yellow sweet pepper (1 large)
- 2 tablespoons olive oil
- 1 tablespoon snipped fresh thyme or ½ teaspoon dried thyme, crushed
- ¼ teaspoon black pepper
- 2 14.5-ounce cans beef or vegetable broth
- ½ cup brown rice or pearl barley

1. Preheat oven to 325°F. To roast garlic, with a sharp knife cut off top ½ inch of the garlic bulb to expose ends of individual cloves. Leaving bulb whole, remove any loose papery outer layers. Fold a 20×18-inch piece of heavy foil in half crosswise. Trim to 10-inch square. Place garlic bulb, cut ends up, in center of foil. Drizzle bulb with the 2 teaspoons olive oil. Bake for 45 to 60 minutes or until the cloves are very soft. Set aside until cool enough to handle. Squeeze garlic paste from individual cloves. Using a fork, mash garlic.
2. Cut off mushroom stems even with caps; discard stems and clean mushrooms. Thinly slice mushroom caps; cut slices into 2-inch pieces.
3. In a large saucepan cook celery and sweet pepper in hot oil over medium-high heat for 3 minutes. Add mushrooms, dried thyme (if using), and pepper. Cook for 3 to 4 minutes or just until vegetables are tender, gently stirring occasionally.
4. Stir in broth; bring to boiling. Stir in mashed garlic and brown rice. Return to boiling; reduce heat. Simmer, covered, about 45 minutes or until rice is tender. Just before serving, stir in fresh thyme (if using).
PER SERVING *152 cal., 6 g fat (1 g sat. fat), 3 mg chol., 375 mg sodium, 20 g carb., 4 g fiber, 5 g pro.*

Manhattan Clam Chowder

PREP 30 minutes   COOK 11 minutes
MAKES 4 servings

- 1 pint shucked clams or two 6½-ounce cans minced clams
- 1 cup chopped celery (2 stalks)
- ⅓ cup chopped onion (1 small)
- ¼ cup chopped carrot (1 small)
- 2 tablespoons olive oil or vegetable oil
- 1 8-ounce bottle clam juice or 1 cup chicken broth
- 2 cups cubed red potatoes (2 medium)
- 1 teaspoon dried thyme, crushed
- ⅛ teaspoon cayenne pepper
- ⅛ teaspoon black pepper
- 1 14½-ounce can diced tomatoes, undrained
- 2 tablespoons cooked bacon pieces or cooked crumbled bacon*

1. Chop fresh clams (if using), reserving juice; set clams aside. Strain clam juice to remove bits of shell. (Or drain canned clams, reserving the juice.) If necessary, add enough water to reserved clam juice to equal 1½ cups. Set clam juice aside.
2. In a large saucepan cook celery, onion, and carrot in hot oil until tender. Stir in the reserved 1½ cups clam juice and the 8 ounces clam juice. Stir in potatoes, thyme, cayenne pepper, and black pepper. Bring to boiling; reduce heat. Simmer, covered, for 10 minutes. Stir in undrained tomatoes, clams, and bacon. Return to boiling; reduce heat. Cook for 1 to 2 minutes or until heated through.
PER SERVING *252 cal., 9 g fat (1 g sat. fat), 41 mg chol., 503 mg sodium, 24 g carb., 3 g fiber, 18 g pro.*
* If cooking the bacon, cook 2 slices, reserving 2 tablespoons drippings. Omit oil. Cook the celery, onion, and carrot in reserved drippings.

PORTOBELLO
MUSHROOM AND
ROASTED GARLIC SOUP

Festive Beginnings

MIX AND MINGLE while you nibble and sip. Serve any of these savory starters alone—or serve a selection as an appetizer buffet that makes a meal. Find the perfect way to start the party with dips, dumplings, sliders, wings, and sparkling beverages.

FIVE-SPICE CHICKEN
WINGS, PAGE 34

MEATBALL SLIDERS

Meatball Sliders

PREP 10 minutes
SLOW COOK 4 hours
MAKES 24 servings

1 large red onion cut into thin
   wedges (1½ cups)
2 12-ounce packages frozen
   cooked Italian meatballs (24)
1 24- to 26-ounce jar marinara or
   pasta sauce (about 2¼ cups)
1 tablespoon balsamic vinegar
½ teaspoon crushed red pepper
6 slices provolone cheese,
   quartered (6 ounces)
4 roma tomatoes, sliced
24 cocktail buns, split and toasted,
   if desired

1. Place onion wedges in a 3½- or
4-quart slow cooker. Top with frozen
meatballs. In a medium bowl combine
marinara sauce, balsamic vinegar,
and crushed red pepper. Pour over
meatballs.
2. Cover and cook on low-heat setting
for 4 to 5 hours or on high-heat setting
for 2 to 2½ hours.
3. Stir meatballs and sauce. Place a
cheese slice and a tomato slice on the
bottom of each cocktail bun. Top each
with two meatballs; add bun tops.
PER SERVING *217 cal., 11 g fat
(5 g sat. fat), 24 mg chol., 516 mg sodium,
20 g carb., 2 g fiber, 10 g pro.*

TUSCAN APPETIZER
SPIEDINI

Tuscan Appetizer Spiedini

PREP 30 minutes
BAKE 4 minutes at 400°F
MAKES 12 servings

¼ cup olive oil
2 tablespoons lemon juice
2 cloves garlic, minced
   Salt
   Black pepper
1 15-ounce can cannellini beans,
   rinsed and drained
¼ cup sliced Spanish olives or
   kalamata olives
1 tablespoon snipped fresh basil
6 ounces Italian bread or ciabatta
4 ounces chunk soppressata or
   dry salami
4 ounces Pecorino cheese, such as
   Pecorino Tuscano
1 6- to 6.5-ounce jar quartered
   marinated artichoke hearts,
   drained
¾ cup grape tomatoes

1. Preheat oven to 400°F. Line a baking
sheet with foil.
2. For dressing, in a screw-top jar
combine oil, lemon juice, and garlic.
Cover and shake well. Season to
taste with salt and pepper. Reserve
2 tablespoons for brushing the kabobs.
3. In a medium bowl combine beans,
olives, and basil. Toss with the
remaining dressing. Cover and chill
until serving.
4. For the spiedini, cut the bread,
soppressata, and Pecorino cheese into
¾- to 1-inch cubes. (Carefully cut

Pecorino cheese so it does not break.)
On twelve 6-inch bamboo skewers*,
thread the bread, soppressata,
Pecorino, artichokes, and tomatoes.
Brush spiedini with the reserved
2 tablespoons dressing, making sure
the bread is evenly coated.
5. Bake for 4 to 5 minutes or just until
bread starts to brown on the edges
(do not let cheese melt too much or it
will fall off). Meanwhile, divide bean
mixture among individual plates or
spoon onto a serving platter. Place one
spiedini on each plate or arrange on
the platter. Serve warm.
PER SERVING *185 cal., 11 g fat
(3 g sat. fat), 16 mg chol., 575 mg sodium,
14 g carb., 2 g fiber, 9 g pro.*
*Tip Soak wooden skewers in water
for 30 minutes before using.

Five-Spice Chicken Wings

PREP 20 minutes
BAKE 20 minutes at 375°F
SLOW COOK 4 hours
MAKES 18 servings

3 pounds chicken wings (about 18)
1 cup bottled plum sauce
2 tablespoons butter, melted
1 teaspoon five-spice powder
  Thin orange wedges and pineapple slices (optional)

1. Use a sharp knife to carefully cut off tips of the wings; discard wing tips. Arrange wing pieces in a single layer in a foil-lined 15×10×1-inch baking pan. Bake for 20 minutes; drain.
2. For the sauce, in a 3½- or 4-quart slow cooker combine plum sauce, melted butter, and five-spice powder. Add wing pieces, stirring to coat.
3. Cover and cook on low-heat setting for 4 to 5 hours or on high-heat setting for 2 to 2½ hours.
4. Serve immediately or keep covered on low-heat setting up to 2 hours. If desired, garnish with orange wedges and pineapple slices.
PER SERVING *88 cal., 6 g fat (2 g sat. fat), 35 mg chol., 41 mg sodium, 3 g carb., 0 g fiber, 6 g pro.*

Buffalo-Style Chicken Wings
Prepare chicken as in Step 1. For sauce, in slow cooker combine 1½ cups hot-style barbecue sauce, 2 tablespoons melted butter, and 1 to 2 teaspoons bottled hot pepper sauce. Add wing pieces, stirring to coat with sauce. Continue as in Step 3. Serve with bottled blue cheese or ranch salad dressing. Omit the fruit garnish.

Asian Dumplings with Pickled Ginger Drizzle

PREP 50 minutes   COOK 6 minutes
STAND 30 minutes   MAKES 14 servings

2 cups chopped Napa cabbage
1 teaspoon salt
1 tablespoon snipped fresh cilantro
2 teaspoons toasted sesame oil
2 teaspoons soy sauce
2 teaspoons rice wine
1 green onion, thinly sliced
1 small serrano chile pepper, seeded and finely chopped*
1 teaspoon grated fresh ginger
¼ teaspoon hot chili-flavor oil
8 ounces ground raw turkey breast
28 to 30 3½-inch-diameter round wonton wrappers
  Nonstick cooking spray
1 recipe Pickled Ginger Drizzle

1. For filling, in a small bowl combine the chopped cabbage and salt; toss to combine. Let cabbage stand at room temperature for 30 minutes. Transfer cabbage to a fine-mesh sieve; press cabbage firmly to remove all excess liquid. Transfer cabbage to a medium bowl. Add cilantro, sesame oil, soy sauce, rice wine, green onion, serrano chile pepper, ginger, and hot chili oil; toss well to combine. Stir in ground turkey breast until combined.
2. For dumplings, line a baking sheet with waxed paper; set aside. Spoon a scant 1 tablespoon filling in the center of one wonton wrapper. (Cover remaining wrappers with a damp cloth to keep them moist.) Lightly brush edges of wrapper with water, fold dumpling in half and press edges together. Repeat with remaining filling and wrappers to make about 28 dumplings, arranging the dumplings, sealed sides up, about ½ inch apart on the prepared baking sheet.
3. Cut a piece of parchment paper to fit inside a steamer basket. Line steamer basket with parchment. Lightly spray parchment with cooking spray. Arrange dumplings in a single layer in steamer basket (work in batches if necessary).
4. Set steamer basket in a wok or large pot over, but not touching, boiling water. Cover and steam about 6 minutes or until dumplings reach 165°F when an instant-read thermometer is inserted into filling. Remove dumplings and arrange on a serving platter. Serve warm drizzled with Pickled Ginger Drizzle.

Pickled Ginger Drizzle In a screw-top jar combine ⅓ cup canola oil; 2 tablespoons white wine vinegar; 2 tablespoons soy sauce; 1 small fresh jalapeño pepper, seeded and finely chopped (see Tip, below); 1 tablespoon sugar; 1 tablespoon liquid from jar of pickled ginger; 1 tablespoon finely chopped pickled ginger; 1 tablespoon lime juice; and 2 teaspoons toasted sesame oil. Cover and shake well.
PER SERVING *132 cal., 7 g fat (1 g sat. fat), 9 mg chol., 522 mg sodium, 11 g carb., 0 g fiber, 6 g pro.*

***Tip** Because chile peppers contain volatile oils that can burn skin and eyes, avoid direct contact with them as much as possible. When working with chile peppers, wear plastic or rubber gloves. If bare hands do touch the peppers, wash hands and nails well with soap and warm water.

FIVE-SPICE CHICKEN WINGS

ASIAN DUMPLINGS
WITH PICKLED GINGER
DRIZZLE

SWEET ONION-
TOMATO TARTLETS

Sweet Onion-Tomato Tartlets

PREP 30 minutes
ROAST 25 minutes at 400°F
BAKE 15 minutes at 400°F
STAND 5 minutes
MAKES 18 servings

    3 cups grape tomatoes
    1 sweet onion, quartered and
       thinly sliced (about 2 cups)
    2 tablespoons olive oil
    1 tablespoon snipped fresh
       rosemary
    ½ teaspoon salt
    ½ teaspoon black pepper
    1 tablespoon sherry vinegar
    1 17.3-ounce package (2 sheets)
       frozen puff pastry sheets,
       thawed
       Manchego or Parmigiano-
       Reggiano cheese, shaved

1. Preheat oven to 400°F. Prick
tomatoes with a fork or the tip of a
sharp knife. In an ungreased
15×10×1-inch baking pan combine
tomatoes, onion, oil, rosemary, salt,
and pepper. Roast for 25 to 30 minutes
or until onion is tender. Remove from
oven. Sprinkle with vinegar; cool.
2. Meanwhile, line a large baking sheet
with parchment paper or foil. On a
lightly floured surface unfold puff
pastry. Using a 3-inch round cookie
cutter, cut pastry into rounds. Place
rounds on the prepared baking sheet.
3. Spoon about 2 tablespoons of the
roasted tomato filling onto each pastry
round. Bake for 15 to 20 minutes or
until edges are puffed and golden
brown. Let stand on baking sheet for
5 minutes before serving. Garnish with
shaved cheese.
PER SERVING *154 cal., 11 g fat*
(0 g sat. fat), 1 mg chol., 196 mg sodium,
13 g carb., 1 g fiber, 2 g pro.

Chipotle Chorizo and Bean Dip

PREP 30 minutes
BAKE 15 minutes at 450°F
MAKES 16 servings

    8 ounces uncooked chorizo
       sausage, casings removed if
       present

    ½ cup chopped onion (1 medium)
    2 cloves garlic, minced
    1 15-ounce can black beans, rinsed
       and drained
    1 14.5-ounce can diced tomatoes,
       undrained
    ¼ cup snipped fresh cilantro
    1 to 2 teaspoons chopped canned
       chipotle peppers in adobo sauce
    1 15-ounce can pinto beans, rinsed
       and drained
    ½ cup shredded Monterey Jack
       cheese with jalapeño peppers
       (2 ounces)
       Lime wedges
       Tortilla chips

1. Preheat oven to 450°F. In a seasoned
or generously greased 8- to 9-inch
cast-iron skillet cook sausage, onion,
and garlic over medium-high heat until
sausage is browned, using a wooden
spoon to break up meat as it cooks.
Remove sausage mixture from skillet;
drain on paper towels.
2. In a medium bowl stir together
sausage mixture, black beans,
tomatoes, cilantro, and chipotle
peppers. In another medium bowl
mash pinto beans; spread in the same
cast-iron skillet. Top with sausage-
tomato mixture and sprinkle with
cheese.
3. Bake for 15 minutes or until cheese
is golden and dip is bubbly. Serve with
tortilla chips and lime wedges.
PER SERVING *127 cal., 7 g fat*
(3 g sat. fat), 16 mg chol., 398 mg sodium,
11 g carb., 3 g fiber, 8 g pro.

**CHIPOTLE CHORIZO
AND BEAN DIP**

Warm Brie with Fig and Pistachio Tapenade

START TO FINISH 15 minutes
BAKE 5 minutes at 350°F
MAKES 8 servings

  1   8-ounce round Brie cheese
  ½   cup dry-roasted pistachio nuts, chopped
  ⅓   cup dried figs, stems removed and chopped
  2   tablespoons honey
  ¼   teaspoon coarse sea salt
      Baked puff pastry squares, baguette slices, crackers, and/or pear or apple slices

1. Preheat oven to 350°F. Place Brie on a baking sheet. Bake for 5 to 7 minutes or just until warmed through. Place warm Brie on a serving platter.
2. Meanwhile, for the tapenade, in a saucepan combine nuts, figs, and honey. Stir over medium-low heat for 1 to 2 minutes or until honey is melted and nuts and figs are evenly coated.

WARM BRIE WITH
FIG AND PISTACHIO
TAPENADE

3. Spoon tapenade over Brie. Sprinkle with sea salt. Serve with baguette slices, crackers, and/or pear or apple slices.
PER SERVING 170 cal., 11 g fat (5 g sat. fat), 28 mg chol., 253 mg sodium, 11 g carb., 1 g fiber, 8 g pro.

Caramelized Onion Dip

PREP 20 minutes COOK 45 minutes
CHILL 4 hours STAND 30 minutes
MAKES 10 servings

  1   tablespoon butter
  1   tablespoon olive oil
  4   medium onions, halved and sliced ½ inch thick
  1   teaspoon salt
  1   teaspoon sugar
  ½   teaspoon cayenne pepper
  2   cloves garlic, minced
  1   8-ounce carton sour cream
  4   ounces cream cheese, softened
  ½   cup mayonnaise
      Sliced green onions (optional)
      Crackers or potato chips

1. In an extra-large skillet heat butter and oil over medium heat until butter is melted. Add onions, salt, and sugar. Reduce heat to medium-low; cook for 40 to 50 minutes or until onions are deep golden brown and caramelized, stirring occasionally. Transfer ⅓ cup of the onions to a small airtight container; cover and chill for at least 4 hours or up to 3 days. Stir cayenne pepper and garlic into onions remaining in skillet. Cook for 5 minutes. Remove from heat; cool slightly. Coarsely chop onions.
2. Meanwhile, in a large bowl use a potato masher to combine sour cream, softened cream cheese, and mayonnaise. Stir in onion-garlic mixture. Transfer to an airtight container. Cover and chill for at least 4 hours or up to 3 days.
3. Let dip stand at room temperature for 30 minutes before serving. Top dip with the ⅓ cup caramelized onions. If desired, garnish with sliced green onions. Serve with crackers or potato chips.
PER SERVING 198 cal., 19 g fat (7 g sat. fat), 30 mg chol., 357 mg sodium, 6 g carb., 1 g fiber, 2 g pro.

Salami Chips with Grainy Mustard Dip

PREP 15 minutes
BAKE 15 minutes at 375°F
CHILL 2 hours MAKES 6 servings

  ¼   cup sour cream
  ¼   cup mayonnaise
  2   tablespoons Dijon mustard
  2   tablespoons grainy mustard
  8   ounces thinly sliced salami

1. For the Grainy Mustard Dip, in a small serving bowl stir together sour cream, mayonnaise, Dijon mustard, and grainy mustard. Cover with plastic wrap and refrigerate for 2 hours.
2. Preheat oven to 375°F. Line two 15×10×1-inch baking pans with parchment paper. Place two oven racks at the center-most positions.
3. Lay the salami slices in a single layer in the baking pans. Bake for 15 minutes or until evenly browned and rigid. Transfer to paper towels to drain and cool. The salami will crisp further as it cools.
4. Arrange the salami chips in a bowl or on a plate with the dip.
PER SERVING 219 cal., 20 g fat (6 g sat. fat), 49 mg chol., 870 mg sodium, 1 g carb., 0 g fiber, 8 g pro.

Moroccan Spiced Olives

PREP 15 minutes COOK 2 minutes
CHILL 4 hours MAKES 12 servings

  3   cups high-quality green olives (about 1 pound)
  1   large lemon
  1¼ cups olive oil
  1   tablespoon coriander seeds
  1   tablespoon cumin seeds
  3   large cloves garlic, thinly sliced
  1   teaspoon crushed red pepper or 3 dried hot chiles, broken in a few pieces

1. Put the olives in a medium bowl. Use a vegetable peeler to remove long narrow strips of zest from the lemon. Add the lemon zest to the olives, then squeeze the juice from the lemon and pour over the olives. Set aside.

TOASTED WALNUTS WITH TART CHERRIES AND ROSEMARY

SALAMI CHIPS WITH GRAINY MUSTARD DIP

MOROCCAN SPICED OLIVES

2. In a small skillet heat ¼ cup of the olive oil over medium-low heat. Add the coriander seeds and cumin seeds and cook for 2 to 3 minutes or until aromatic and just lightly browned, stirring often. Pour the spices and their oil over the olives. Add the remaining 1 cup olive oil, garlic, and crushed red pepper; stir gently to mix. Cover the bowl and refrigerate for 4 hours or up to 7 days, stirring twice each day.

3. About 1 hour before serving, place olives in one large serving bowl or several small serving bowls. Set out a small dish for olive pits.

PER SERVING *78 cal., 8 g fat (1 g sat. fat), 0 mg chol., 573 mg sodium, 2 g carb., 1 g fiber, 1 g pro.*

Toasted Walnuts with Tart Cherries and Rosemary

PREP **15 minutes**
BAKE **12 minutes at 350°F**
MAKES **12 servings**

2½ cups walnut halves
2 tablespoons unsalted butter, melted
2 tablespoons finely minced fresh rosemary
1 teaspoon kosher salt or flaky or coarse sea salt
½ teaspoon freshly ground black pepper
¾ cup dried tart cherries

1. Preheat oven to 350°F. Place the walnuts in a medium bowl; drizzle with butter. Toss to coat. Add the rosemary, salt, and pepper; toss to mix.

2. Spread the nuts in a 15×10×1-inch baking pan. Bake for 12 to 14 minutes or until lightly browned and fragrant, stirring once halfway through baking.

3. Transfer the nuts to a medium bowl, add the dried cherries, and toss to mix. Serve warm, or cool and store in an airtight container up to 5 days.

PER SERVING *161 cal., 14 g fat (2 g sat. fat), 5 mg chol., 153 mg sodium, 10 g carb., 2 g fiber, 3 g pro.*

POMEGRANATE-
ORANGE WINE
SPRITZER

Pomegranate-Orange Wine Spritzer

PREP 15 minutes CHILL 2 hours
MAKES 12 servings

- 1 750-milliliter bottle sweet white wine (such as Gewurztraminer or Riesling), chilled
- 2 cups pomegranate juice, chilled
- 1 orange, halved and thinly sliced
- 2 12-ounce bottles sparkling water, chilled
  Orange peel twists (optional)

1. In a large pitcher combine wine, pomegranate juice, and orange slices. Cover and chill for 2 to 6 hours.
2. To serve, slowly pour sparkling water into wine mixture, stirring just until combined. Pour into glasses. If desired, garnish with orange peel twists.
PER SERVING *78 cal., 0 g fat, 0 mg chol., 0 mg sodium, 8 g carb., 0 g fiber, 0 g pro.*

Cheddar-Blue Thumbprints

PREP 30 minutes
BAKE 13 minutes at 350°F
COOL 15 minutes
MAKES 42 servings

- 1½ cups shredded white cheddar cheese or extra-sharp cheddar cheese (6 ounces)
- ½ cup finely shredded Parmesan cheese (2 ounces)
- ½ cup butter, softened
- 1 egg yolk
- ¼ teaspoon black pepper
- 1 cup all-purpose flour
- 1 egg white
- 1 tablespoon water
- 1¼ cups finely chopped almonds, lightly toasted (see tip, page 19)
- ⅓ cup seedless raspberry preserves
- 4 ounces blue cheese, cut into small cubes

1. Preheat oven to 350°F. Line a cookie sheet with parchment paper or lightly grease a cookie sheet; set aside. In a food processor combine cheddar cheese, Parmesan cheese, and butter. Cover and process until well mixed. Add egg yolk and pepper; cover and process until combined. Add flour; cover and process with on/off pulses until a soft dough forms. (Or in a medium mixing bowl beat butter with an electric mixer on medium to high for 30 seconds. Beat in cheddar cheese and Parmesan cheese until combined. Beat in egg yolk and pepper. Beat in flour until a soft dough forms.)
2. In a small bowl combine egg white and the water. Place almonds in a shallow dish. Shape dough into forty-two ¾-inch balls. Roll balls in egg white mixture, then in almonds to coat. Place 1 inch apart on the prepared cookie sheet. Press your thumb into the center of each ball, reshaping as necessary.
3. Bake for 10 minutes or until edges are firm and cookies are light brown. If cookie centers puff during baking, indent with the back of a small spoon. Spoon preserves into indentations of cookies. Top each cookie with a cube of blue cheese. Bake for 3 to 4 minutes or until cheese is softened.
4. Transfer cookies to a wire rack; cool for 15 minutes before serving. Cover and chill within 2 hours.
PER SERVING *87 cal., 6 g fat (3 g sat. fat), 17 mg chol., 101 mg sodium, 5 g carb., 1 g fiber, 3 g pro.*

Apple-Cinnamon Winter Sangria

PREP 15 minutes CHILL 24 hours
MAKES 8 servings

- ½ cup dried apples
- ½ cup dried cranberries
- ½ cup raisins
- 6 dried apricots, cut into slivers
- ¼ cup brandy
- 2 tablespoons honey
- ½ vanilla bean, slit lengthwise
- 1 2¾-inch stick cinnamon
- 1 750-milliliter bottle Merlot
- 2 cups club soda
  Ice cubes

1. In a large saucepan stir together the apples, cranberries, raisins, apricots, brandy, honey, vanilla bean, and cinnamon. Stir until mixture comes to a gentle boil. Remove from heat; cool slightly. Stir in wine. Transfer to a pitcher. Cover and chill up to 24 hours to blend flavors.
2. Just before serving, strain fruit from sangria. Stir in club soda. Layer fruit and ice in glasses. Pour sangria into glasses.
PER SERVING *199 cal., 0 g fat, 0 mg chol., 52 mg sodium, 29 g carb., 1 g fiber, 1 g pro.*

**APPLE-CINNAMON
WINTER SANGRIA**

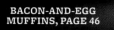

**BACON-AND-EGG
MUFFINS, PAGE 46**

Sweet and Savory Brunch

START THE DAY with a festive holiday spread. Build a brunch with these recipes for eggs, hearty meat dishes, pancakes, French toast, fruit salad, green salad—and beautiful breads of all kinds.

MAPLE-APPLE GLAZED
BREAKFAST MEATBALLS

Maple-Apple Glazed Breakfast Meatballs

PREP 40 minutes
BAKE 10 minutes at 400°F
MAKES 8 servings

Nonstick cooking spray
1 egg
½ cup quick-cooking oats
1 small red-skinned cooking apple, cored and finely chopped (about ½ cup)
2 teaspoons snipped fresh sage or ½ teaspoon dried sage, crushed
¾ teaspoon fennel seeds, crushed
½ teaspoon salt
⅛ teaspoon black pepper
1 pound ground pork
¼ cup apple jelly
¼ cup pure maple syrup
Fresh sage (optional)

1. Preheat oven to 400°F. Line a 15×10×1-inch baking pan with foil. Lightly coat foil with cooking spray; set aside. For the meatballs, in a bowl beat egg lightly with a fork. Stir in oats, apple, sage, fennel seeds, salt, and pepper. Add pork; mix until combined.
2. Shape meat mixture into forty 1-inch meatballs. Place meatballs in prepared baking pan, spacing ½ inch apart.
3. Bake meatballs for 8 to 10 minutes or until cooked through (160°F).
4. Meanwhile, for the Maple-Apple Glaze, in a small saucepan heat and whisk jelly and maple syrup over medium-low heat until jelly is melted and mixture is smooth. Drizzle ¼ cup of the glaze over baked meatballs, lightly toss, and bake meatballs 2 minutes more.
5. Transfer meatballs to a serving platter. Drizzle with remaining ¼ cup glaze. If desired, garnish with fresh sage.
PER SERVING 232 cal., 12 g fat (5 g sat. fat), 64 mg chol., 191 mg sodium, 19 g carb., 1 g fiber, 11 g pro.

PORK AND HOT PEPPER HASH

Pork and Hot Pepper Hash

PREP 20 minutes STAND 15 minutes
COOK 20 minutes MAKES 4 servings

1 cup loosely packed fresh cilantro leaves, finely chopped
1 poblano pepper, seeded and finely chopped (see tip, page 34)
1 jalapeño, seeded and finely chopped (see tip, page 34)
1 clove garlic, minced
1¼ pounds ground pork
3 tablespoons lime juice
1 pound baby Yukon gold potatoes, halved or quartered
½ teaspoon salt
¼ teaspoon black pepper and/or crushed red pepper
¼ cup chicken broth (optional)
1 tablespoon butter
4 eggs
Sliced red and/or green jalapeños (optional) (see Tip, page 34)
Fresh cilantro sprigs (optional)
Bottled green hot pepper sauce
Lime wedges

1. In a large bowl combine cilantro, poblano, jalapeño, and garlic. Add pork and lime juice. Gently mix to combine. Let stand for 15 minutes to blend flavors.
2. Meanwhile, in a large saucepan cook potatoes in boiling salted water, covered, for about 10 minutes or just until tender. Drain.
3. In a large skillet cook pork mixture until pork begins to brown. Stir in potatoes; sprinkle with salt and pepper. Cook 5 to 7 minutes more or until pork is cooked through and potatoes are tender, turning occasionally. For more moist hash, stir in chicken broth, if desired.
4. In a large skillet melt the 1 tablespoon butter over medium heat. Break eggs into skillet. Reduce heat to low; cook for 3 to 4 minutes or until whites are completely set and yolks start to thicken.
5. Serve eggs over hash. Top with sliced peppers and additional cilantro, if desired. Pass bottled green hot pepper sauce and lime wedges.
PER SERVING 500 cal., 33 g fat (15 g sat. fat), 110 mg chol., 418 mg sodium, 24 g carb., 3.6 g fiber, 27 g pro.

Goat Cheese, Artichoke, and Smoked Ham Strata

PREP 30 minutes STAND 20 minutes
CHILL 2 hours BAKE 1 hour at 350°F
MAKES 8 servings

- 2 cups whole milk
- 2 tablespoons olive oil
- 1 1-pound loaf sourdough bread, cut into 1-inch cubes (about 12 cups)
- 5 eggs
- 1½ cups half-and-half or light cream
- 1 tablespoon minced garlic
- 1½ teaspoons herbes de Provence
- ¾ teaspoon black pepper
- ½ teaspoon freshly ground nutmeg
- ½ teaspoon dried sage, crushed
- ½ teaspoon dried thyme, crushed
- 8 ounces goat cheese (chèvre), crumbled (1 cup)
- 12 ounces smoked ham, chopped
- 3 6-ounce jars marinated artichoke hearts, drained and halved lengthwise
- 6 ounces Parmesan cheese, finely shredded (1½ cups)
- 4 ounces fontina cheese, shredded (1 cup)

1. Grease a 3-quart rectangular baking dish; set aside. In an extra-large bowl combine milk and olive oil. Add bread cubes, stirring to coat. Let stand for 10 minutes.

2. In a large bowl whisk together eggs, half-and-half, garlic, herbes de Provence, pepper, nutmeg, sage, and thyme. Whisk in goat cheese until combined; set aside.

3. Spread half the bread cube mixture in the prepared dish. Top with half each of the ham, artichoke hearts, and cheeses. Repeat layers. Drizzle egg mixture over all. Cover and chill for 2 to 24 hours.

4. Preheat oven to 350°F. Uncover and bake for 1 hour or until center is set and edges are browned. Let stand for 10 minutes before serving.

PER SERVING *693 cal., 38 g fat (19 g sat. fat), 218 mg chol., 1,661 mg sodium, 47 g carb., 3 g fiber, 41 g pro.*

Bacon-and-Egg Muffins

(photo page 42)

PREP 30 minutes
BAKE 15 minutes at 400°F
COOL 5 minutes MAKES 12 servings

- 4 slices bacon, cut into thirds
- 5 eggs
- 2 tablespoons water
  Salt and black pepper
- 1 cup all-purpose flour
- ½ cup yellow cornmeal
- 2 tablespoons sugar
- 2½ teaspoons baking powder
- ½ teaspoon salt
- 1 cup milk
- ¼ cup vegetable oil or melted butter
- ½ cup shredded cheddar cheese (4 ounces)
  Maple syrup (optional)

1. Preheat oven to 400°F. In a large skillet cook bacon just until it begins to crisp. Drain and reserve drippings. Return 2 teaspoons drippings to skillet. For scrambled eggs, in a small bowl beat 3 of the eggs, the water, and a dash each of salt and pepper. Cook eggs in hot skillet over medium heat without stirring until eggs begin to set on bottom and around edges. With a large spatula, lift and fold partially cooked eggs so the uncooked portion flows underneath. Cook through just until glossy and moist. Transfer to small bowl; set aside.

2. Brush twelve 2½-inch muffin cups with some of the remaining bacon drippings. Set muffin cups aside. In a medium bowl stir together flour, cornmeal, sugar, baking powder, and the ½ teaspoon salt. Make a well in center of flour mixture. In a separate bowl combine milk, oil, and the remaining 2 eggs. Add egg mixture all at once to flour mixture. Stir just until moistened (batter should be lumpy). Fold in scrambled eggs and cheese. Spoon batter into muffin cups (cups will be full). Place one bacon piece on each muffin.

3. Bake for 15 to 17 minutes or until light brown and a wooden toothpick inserted in centers comes out clean. Cool in cups on a wire rack for 5 minutes. To loosen muffins, run a small metal spatula or table knife around edges of muffins; remove from muffin cups. If desired, serve warm with maple syrup.

PER SERVING *202 cal., 12 g fat (3 g sat. fat), 89 mg chol., 356 mg sodium, 16 g carb., 1 g fiber, 7 g pro.*

GOAT CHEESE, ARTICHOKE, AND SMOKED HAM STRATA

EGGS AND GREENS
BREAKFAST PIZZA

Eggs and Greens
Breakfast Pizza

PREP 25 minutes STAND 30 minutes
BAKE 4 minutes at 400°F /
12 minutes at 450°F
MAKES 4 servings

4   eggs
8   ounces hot or sweet Italian
    sausage (remove casings if
    present)
4   7-inch Greek flatbread or pita
    bread rounds
1   cup pizza sauce or thick
    marinara sauce
½   cup shredded mozzarella cheese
    (2 ounces)
½   cup shredded cheddar cheese
    (2 ounces)
½   cup thinly sliced red onion

4   cups torn arugula
1   tablespoon olive oil
1   teaspoon lemon juice
⅛   teaspoon salt
⅛   teaspoon black pepper
1   to 2 tablespoons shaved
    Parmesan cheese

1. Let eggs stand at room temperature
for 30 minutes. Preheat oven to 400°F.
Line a baking sheet with foil; set aside.
In a large skillet cook sausage over
medium heat until browned, using a
wooden spoon to break up meat as it
cooks. Drain off fat.
2. Meanwhile, place flatbreads directly
on oven rack. Heat for 4 to 6 minutes
or until lightly toasted, turning once.
Arrange flatbreads on the prepared
baking sheet. Increase oven to 450°F.

3. Spread one-fourth of the pizza
sauce on each flatbread. Sprinkle
with mozzarella and cheddar cheeses,
cooked sausage, and onion. For each
pizza, break an egg into a small dish*;
make a small indentation in the center
of one pizza and pour the egg into the
indentation. Bake for 12 to 15 minutes
or until egg whites are set and yolks
begin to thicken.
4. In a medium bowl toss together
arugula, oil, lemon juice, salt, and
pepper. Top pizzas with arugula,
sprinkle with shaved Parmesan.
PER SERVING *593 cal., 30 g fat
(12 g sat. fat), 250 mg chol., 1,122 mg sodium,
45 g carb., 3 g fiber, 30 g pro.*
*Tip If the yolk cracks when you break
the egg, start over with another egg.

FRESH MOZZARELLA SALAD

enough to handle. Using a sharp knife, loosen edges of skins; gently pull off skins in strips and discard.

2. Cut roasted sweet peppers into 3×1½-inch strips. For vinaigrette, in a glass measuring cup whisk together olive oil and balsamic vinegar. Divide vinaigrette among four chilled salad plates. Top with greens, cheese, and roasted peppers. Sprinkle with pepper and, if desired, salt.

3. Surround with the remaining arugula.

PER SERVING *306 cal., 26 g fat (9 g sat. fat), 44 mg chol., 218 mg sodium, 8 g carb., 0 g fiber, 12 g pro.*

Quinoa-Pumpkin Seed Granola

PREP **20 minutes**
BAKE **20 minutes at 350°F**
MAKES **13 servings**

- ¾ cup uncooked quinoa, rinsed and well-drained
- ½ cup raw pumpkin seeds (pepitas)
- ½ cup whole and/or slivered almonds
- ¼ cup flaxseeds
- ¼ cup honey
- 2 tablespoons canola oil
- 1 teaspoon ground cinnamon
- ½ teaspoon coarse salt
- ¾ cup dried cherries, cranberries, golden raisins, and/or snipped dried apricots

1. Preheat oven to 350°F. In a large bowl combine quinoa, pumpkin seeds, almonds, and flaxseeds. In a small microwave-safe bowl heat honey on high for 20 seconds. Stir in oil, cinnamon, and salt. Pour honey mixture over quinoa mixture; toss to coat. Spread in a 15×10×1-inch baking pan.

2. Bake, uncovered, for 20 minutes or until golden, stirring twice. Stir in dried fruit. Cool for 15 minutes in the pan. Spread out on foil. Cool completely, breaking up any large pieces. Transfer to an airtight container to store. Makes 3¼ cups granola.

PER SERVING *191 cal., 11 g fat (1 g sat. fat), 0 mg chol., 94 mg sodium, 22 g carb., 3 g fiber, 6 g pro.*

Fresh Mozzarella Salad

PREP **25 minutes**
ROAST **20 minutes at 425°F**
STAND **30 minutes**
MAKES **4 servings**

- 2 medium red and/or yellow sweet peppers
- 8 ounces fresh mozzarella cheese, sliced, or smoked fresh mozzarella cheese
- 2 cups fresh arugula or spinach
- ¼ cup olive oil
- ¼ cup balsamic vinegar
- ¼ teaspoon coarsely ground black pepper
- ⅛ teaspoon salt (optional)

1. Preheat oven to 425°F. Halve sweet peppers lengthwise; remove stems, seeds, and membranes. Place peppers, cut sides down, on a foil-lined baking sheet. Roast for 20 to 25 minutes or until peppers are charred and very tender. Bring foil up around peppers and fold edges together to enclose. Let stand about 30 minutes or until cool

Greek Yogurt and Cornflakes Tart

PREP 35 minutes
BAKE 8 minutes at 350°F
CHILL 4 hours MAKES 8 servings

1½ cups crushed cornflakes (about 5 cups whole flakes)
⅓ cup butter, melted
3 tablespoons packed brown sugar
1 envelope unflavored gelatin
¼ cup water
1¼ cups plain Greek yogurt
½ cup milk
¼ cup honey
1 teaspoon vanilla
4 small oranges or clementines or 2 medium oranges
¼ cup orange marmalade

1. Preheat oven to 350°F. In a medium bowl combine cornflakes, melted butter, and brown sugar. Press into the bottom and up the sides of a 14×5×1-inch or 11×8×1-inch fluted tart pan with removable bottom. Bake for 8 to 10 minutes or until golden brown. Cool on a wire rack.

2. Meanwhile, in a 1-cup glass measure sprinkle gelatin over the water; let stand several minutes to soften. Heat in a microwave oven on high for 20 seconds or until gelatin is dissolved, stirring twice. In a large bowl whisk together yogurt, milk, honey, and vanilla; whisk in dissolved gelatin. Pour yogurt mixture over prepared crust. Chill for 4 to 24 hours.

3. Peel and thinly slice oranges. Remove and discard seeds.

4. Remove tart from pan; sprinkle loose crust pieces on edges of tart. Arrange orange slices on tart. In a small saucepan, heat marmalade just until melted; brush or drizzle on oranges. Cut crosswise to serve.

PER SERVING *298 cal., 11 g fat (7 g sat. fat), 34 mg chol., 224 mg sodium, 42 g carb., 2 g fiber, 10 g pro.*

GREEK YOGURT AND CORNFLAKES TART

NUTS ABOUT FRENCH TOAST

Orange Ricotta Pancakes

START TO FINISH 30 minutes
MAKES 5 servings

    1 recipe Raspberry Orange Syrup
 1½ cups all-purpose flour
  ½ cup cornmeal
    2 tablespoons sugar
    1 teaspoon baking powder
  ½ teaspoon baking soda
  ½ teaspoon salt
    1 cup milk
  ½ cup ricotta cheese
  ¼ cup orange juice
    2 eggs
    2 teaspoons finely shredded
        orange peel
        Butter
        Fresh raspberries
        Powdered sugar (optional)

1. For pancakes, in a large mixing bowl combine flour, cornmeal, sugar, baking powder, baking soda, and salt. In a medium bowl whisk together milk, cheese, orange juice, eggs, and orange peel. Add milk mixture to flour mixture; stir just until combined.
2. Preheat a griddle over medium heat; brush lightly with butter. Add ¼ to ⅓ cup batter per pancake. Cook about 2 minutes; turn over when surfaces are bubbly and edges are slightly dry. Cook 1 to 2 minutes more or until done.
3. Pour Raspberry-Orange Syrup over pancakes. Serve with additional fresh raspberries. Sprinkle with powdered sugar, if desired.
Raspberry Orange Syrup In a blender puree 1 cup sugar, ½ cup orange juice, 1 tablespoon lemon juice, and 1 pint raspberries. Strain puree through a fine-mesh sieve; place in a small saucepan. In a cup whisk together 1 tablespoon water and 2 teaspoons cornstarch; gradually whisk into the puree in pan. Cook, whisking constantly, over medium heat until thickened and bubbly. Cook and whisk for 2 minutes more.
PER SERVING *527 cal., 9 g fat (5 g sat. fat), 97 mg chol., 551 mg sodium, 99 g carb., 5 g fiber, 13 g pro.*

Nuts About French Toast

PREP 25 minutes CHILL overnight
BAKE 1 hour at 325°F
STAND 15 minutes
MAKES 10 servings

 12 ounces Italian bread, cut into
        1-inch slices
    8 eggs, lightly beaten
    2 cups milk
    2 cups half-and-half or light cream
    2 teaspoons vanilla
  ½ teaspoon ground nutmeg
  ½ teaspoon ground cinnamon
  ½ cup butter, softened
    1 cup packed brown sugar
    2 tablespoons dark-color corn syrup
    1 cup coarsely chopped pecans,
        walnuts, hickory, and/or
        hazelnuts
        Chopped nuts (optional)

1. Butter a 13×9×2-inch baking dish. Arrange bread slices in the dish, overlapping as necessary.
2. In a large mixing bowl combine eggs, milk, half-and-half, vanilla, nutmeg, and cinnamon. Slowly pour egg mixture evenly over bread. Press down lightly with a large spoon. Cover and chill in the refrigerator overnight.
3. Preheat oven to 325°F. For the topping, in a medium bowl mix together butter, brown sugar, and corn syrup. Stir in nuts. Spoon small mounds of topping over the bread.
4. Place the baking dish in a 15×10×1-inch baking pan to catch drips during baking. Bake, uncovered, for 1 hour or until puffed and golden. Let stand 15 minutes. If desired, sprinkle with additional chopped nuts.
PER SERVING *492 cal., 29 g fat (12 g sat. fat), 215 mg chol., 372 mg sodium, 48 g carb., 2 g fiber, 12 g pro.*

ORANGE RICOTTA
PANCAKES

**LEMON-HONEY
SWEET ROLLS**

Lemon-Honey
Sweet Rolls

PREP **45 minutes**
RISE **1 hour 30 minutes**
BAKE **25 minutes at 350°F**
MAKES **15 servings**

1¼ cups warm water (105°F to 115°F)
 2 packages active dry yeast
 2 eggs, lightly beaten
 ½ cup nonfat dry milk powder
 ⅓ cup butter, softened
 ⅓ cup honey
 2 tablespoons toasted wheat germ
 1 teaspoon salt
 2 cups bread flour
2½ to 3 cups white whole wheat
   flour or all-purpose flour
 1 cup golden raisins
 ¼ cup butter, softened
 ¼ cup honey
 2 teaspoons finely shredded lemon
   peel
 1 recipe Lemon Icing

1. In a large mixing bowl stir together the warm water and yeast; let stand about 5 minutes or until yeast is dissolved. Add eggs, dry milk powder, the ⅓ cup butter, the ⅓ cup honey, wheat germ, and salt. Beat with a mixer on low to medium for 30 seconds, scraping sides of bowl constantly. Add bread flour. Beat on low to medium for 30 seconds, scraping sides of bowl constantly. Beat on high for 3 minutes. Using a wooden spoon, stir in as much of the white whole wheat flour as you can.
2. Turn dough out onto a lightly floured surface. Knead in enough of the remaining white whole wheat flour to make a moderately soft dough that is smooth and elastic (3 to 5 minutes total). Shape dough into a ball. Place in a lightly greased bowl, turning once to grease surface of dough. Cover and let rise in a warm place until double in size (about 1 hour).

3. Punch dough down. Turn out onto a lightly floured surface. Cover and let rest for 10 minutes. Meanwhile, lightly grease a 13×9×2-inch baking pan; set aside.
4. In a small bowl combine raisins and enough warm water to cover. Let stand for 5 minutes; drain well. For filling, in a medium bowl combine the ¼ cup butter, ¼ cup honey, and lemon peel until smooth.
5. Roll dough into an 18×15-inch rectangle. Spread filling evenly over dough to within 1 inch along the long sides. Sprinkle raisins on filling. Roll up, starting from a long side; pinch dough to seal seam. Slice roll into 15 pieces. Arrange pieces in the prepared baking pan. Cover and let rise in a warm place until nearly double in size (about 30 minutes).
6. Preheat oven to 350°F. Bake for 25 minutes or until golden. Cool in pan for 1 minute. Carefully invert rolls onto a wire rack; cool slightly. Invert again onto a serving platter. Drizzle with Lemon Icing.
Lemon Icing In a small bowl combine 2 cups powdered sugar, 2 teaspoons finely shredded lemon peel, and 3 tablespoons lemon juice. Stir in enough additional lemon juice to make an icing of drizzling consistency.
PER SERVING *363 cal., 8 g fat (5 g sat. fat), 45 mg chol., 252 mg sodium, 67 g carb., 3 g fiber, 8 g pro.*

Pecan Browned-Butter Coffee Cake

PREP 35 minutes   CHILL 2 hours
BAKE 50 minutes at 325°F
COOL 1 hour   MAKES 12 servings

¾ cup butter
2 cups pecan halves or pieces, toasted and finely chopped (see tip, page 19)
2 cups packed brown sugar
2 teaspoons all-purpose flour
3 cups all-purpose flour
1½ teaspoons baking powder
1½ teaspoons baking soda
¾ teaspoon salt
3 eggs
1 teaspoon vanilla
1½ cups plain yogurt
1 recipe Coffee Icing

1. In a medium saucepan melt butter over medium heat. Reduce heat to medium-low. Cook, without stirring, for 5 to 6 minutes or until butter becomes brown and fragrant. Remove from heat; cool slightly. Transfer to a small bowl. Cover and chill for 2 hours or freeze for 30 minutes or until firm.
2. Preheat oven to 325°F. Grease and flour a 10-inch fluted tube pan or coat with nonstick spray for baking; set aside. For filling, in a small bowl combine ¾ cup of the pecans, ½ cup of the brown sugar, and the 2 teaspoons flour. Add 3 tablespoons of the browned butter and work in with fingers or a fork until mixture is crumbly; set aside. In a medium bowl stir together the 3 cups flour, the baking powder, baking soda, and salt.
3. In a large mixing bowl beat remaining browned butter with a mixer on medium to high for 30 seconds. Add remaining 1½ cups brown sugar; beat until combined, scraping sides of bowl occasionally. Add eggs, one at a time, beating after each addition until combined. Stir in vanilla. Alternately add flour mixture and yogurt to butter mixture, beating on low after each addition just until combined. Stir in remaining 1¼ cups pecans.
4. Spoon half the batter into prepared pan, spreading evenly. Sprinkle batter in pan evenly with filling. Spoon remaining batter over filling, spreading to cover.
5. Bake for 50 minutes or until a toothpick inserted near the center comes out clean. Cool in pan on a wire rack for 10 minutes. Remove from pan. Cool about 45 minutes before serving. Drizzle with Coffee Icing.
Coffee Icing In a small bowl stir together 4 teaspoons milk and 1 teaspoon instant coffee crystals until coffee is dissolved. Stir in 1 cup powdered sugar and enough additional milk, 1 teaspoon at a time, to make icing a drizzling consistency.
PER SERVING *561 cal., 27 g fat (9 g sat. fat), 85 mg chol., 481 mg sodium, 75 g carb., 3 g fiber, 8 g pro.*

Apple-Streusel Muffins

PREP 25 minutes
BAKE 18 minutes at 375°F
COOL 5 minutes   MAKES 12 servings

Nonstick cooking spray
1 cup all-purpose flour
1 cup whole wheat flour or white whole wheat flour
⅓ cup packed brown sugar
2½ teaspoons baking powder
1 teaspoon apple pie spice
¼ teaspoon salt
2 eggs, lightly beaten
1 cup buttermilk
2 tablespoons canola oil
¾ cup shredded peeled apple (1 medium)
2 tablespoons finely chopped pecans
1 tablespoon flaxseed meal or toasted wheat germ
1 tablespoon packed brown sugar
1 tablespoon butter

1. Preheat oven to 375°F. Lightly coat twelve 2½-inch muffin cups with cooking spray or line with paper bake cups and coat bake cups with cooking spray; set aside. In a large bowl stir together all-purpose flour, whole wheat flour, ⅓ cup brown sugar, baking powder, apple pie spice, and salt. Make a well in the center of flour mixture; set aside.
2. In a medium bowl combine eggs, buttermilk, and oil. Add egg mixture all at once to flour mixture. Stir just until moistened (batter should be lumpy). Fold in shredded apple. Spoon batter into the prepared muffin cups, filling each about three-fourths full.
3. For topping, in a small bowl combine pecans, flaxseed meal, and 1 tablespoon brown sugar. Using a pastry blender, cut in butter until mixture resembles coarse crumbs. Spoon topping onto batter in cups.
4. Bake for 18 to 20 minutes or until a wooden toothpick inserted in the centers comes out clean. Cool in muffin cups on a wire rack for 5 minutes. Remove muffins from muffin cups. Serve warm.
PER SERVING *163 cal., 6 g fat (1 g sat. fat), 39 mg chol., 167 mg sodium, 25 g carb., 2 g fiber, 4 g pro.*

PECAN BROWNED-BUTTER COFFEE CAKE

APPLE-STREUSEL
MUFFINS

CRANBERRY-
CHOCOLATE SCONES

Cranberry-Chocolate Scones

PREP 20 minutes
BAKE 12 minutes at 400°F
MAKES 12 servings

2½ cups all-purpose flour
 2 tablespoons sugar
 1 tablespoon baking powder
 ¼ teaspoon salt
 ⅓ cup butter
 2 eggs, lightly beaten
 ¾ cup whipping cream
 ¼ cup chopped dried cranberries
 ¼ cup miniature semisweet
   chocolate pieces
 ½ teaspoon finely shredded orange
   peel (optional)
   Whipping cream or milk
 1 recipe Orange Drizzle

1. Preheat oven to 400°F. In a large bowl stir together flour, sugar, baking powder, and salt. Using a pastry blender, cut in butter until mixture resembles coarse crumbs. Make a well in the center of flour mixture; set aside.
2. In a medium bowl combine eggs, ¾ cup whipping cream, dried cranberries, chocolate pieces, and, if desired, orange peel. Add egg mixture all at once to flour mixture. Using a fork, stir just until moistened.
3. Turn dough out onto a lightly floured surface. Knead by folding and gently pressing dough for 10 to 12 strokes or until nearly smooth. Divide dough in half. Pat or lightly roll each portion into a 6-inch circle. Cut each circle into six wedges.
4. Place dough wedges 2 inches apart on an ungreased baking sheet. Brush with additional whipping cream.
5. Bake for 12 to 14 minutes or until golden. Cool slightly on baking sheet. Drizzle with Orange Drizzle. Serve warm or at room temperature.
Orange Drizzle In a small bowl combine 1 cup powdered sugar, 1 tablespoon orange juice, and ¼ teaspoon vanilla. Stir in additional orange juice, 1 teaspoon at a time, to reach a drizzling consistency.
PER SERVING *291 cal., 14 g fat (8 g sat. fat), 67 mg chol., 203 mg sodium, 38 g carb., 1 g fiber, 4 g pro.*

MOCHA COFFEE COOLER

Mocha Coffee Cooler

START TO FINISH 5 minutes
MAKES 4 servings

 1 cup strong coffee, chilled
 1 cup half-and-half, light cream, . or milk
 3 tablespoons chocolate-flavor syrup
 2 tablespoons sugar
 1 cup ice cubes
   Additional chocolate-flavor syrup (optional)
   Crushed chocolate-covered coffee beans (optional)

1. In a blender combine coffee, half-and-half, chocolate syrup, and sugar. Cover and blend until combined. Add ice cubes; cover and blend until nearly smooth. If desired, drizzle chocolate syrup inside glasses. Pour mocha into glasses. If desired, top with crushed coffee beans.
PER SERVING *142 cal., 7 g fat (4 g sat. fat), 22 mg chol., 36 mg sodium, 18 g carb., 0 g fiber, 2 g pro.*

Carrot-Clementine Agua Fresca

START TO FINISH 20 minutes
MAKES 6 servings

 3 pounds packaged peeled fresh baby carrots
 6 clementines or tangerines, peeled, seeded, and chopped
 3 cups cold water
 2 tablespoons lime juice
 2 tablespoons honey
   Honey (optional)
   Ice cubes
   Clementine slices

1. In a blender combine about 1 pound of the carrots, 2 of the clementines, and 1 cup of the water. Cover and blend until smooth. Strain through a fine-mesh sieve into a pitcher, discarding solids. Repeat twice.
2. Stir lime juice and the 2 tablespoons honey into agua fresca. If desired, add additional honey to taste.
3. Serve over ice. Garnish with clementine slices.
PER SERVING *152 cal., 1 g fat (0 g sat. fat), 0 mg chol., 162 mg sodium, 37 g carb., 8 g fiber, 3 g pro.*

BEST BASIC CHALLAH,
PAGE 60

Scratch Bread

AMIDST THE HUSTLE and bustle of the holidays, slow down for just a while to stir up some homemade bread. The smell of it baking in the oven is heavenly, the satisfaction of having made it is pure joy—it simply makes the season more special.

Best Basic Challah

(photo page 58)

PREP 1 hour STAND 10 minutes
RISE 1 hour 30 minutes
BAKE 30 minutes at 350°F
MAKES 48 servings

1¾ cups warm water (105°F to 115°F)
½ cup honey
2 packages active dry yeast
4 eggs, lightly beaten
½ cup butter, melted and cooled
1 tablespoon salt
7½ to 8 cups bread flour
1 egg, lightly beaten
1 tablespoon water

1. In a large bowl stir together the 1¾ cups warm water, the honey, and yeast. Let stand about 10 minutes or until yeast is foamy. Using a wooden spoon, stir in the 4 eggs, the melted butter, and salt. Gradually stir in as much of the flour as you can.
2. Turn dough out onto a lightly floured surface. Knead in enough of the remaining flour to make a moderately soft dough that is smooth and elastic (5 to 7 minutes total). Shape dough into a ball. Place in a lightly greased bowl, turning once to grease surface of dough. Cover; let rise in a warm place until double in size (1 to 1½ hours).
3. Punch dough down. Turn dough out onto a lightly floured surface. Divide into six portions. Cover; let rest for 10 minutes. Meanwhile, lightly grease a large baking sheet; set aside.
4. Divide each portion into thirds (18 portions total). Gently roll each third into an 18-inch-long rope. Place three ropes on the prepared baking sheet 1 inch apart; braid. Repeat with another three ropes to make another braid. Brush one side of a braid with water; lightly press the two braids together to make a double-braided loaf. Repeat with remaining portions of dough to make two more double-braided loaves. Cover and let rise in a warm place until nearly double in size (about 30 minutes).
5. Preheat oven to 350°F. In a small bowl combine the 1 egg and the 1 tablespoon water; brush over braids. Bake for 30 to 35 minutes or until loaves sound hollow when lightly tapped. Immediately remove loaves from baking sheet. Cool on wire racks.

PER SERVING 113 cal., 3 g fat (1 g sat. fat), 27 mg chol., 167 mg sodium, 19 g carb., 1 g fiber, 3 g pro.

Tip For extra-glossy loaves, remove from oven and immediately brush with additional egg mixture.

Garlic-Herb Challah Prepare as directed, except reduce honey to 2 tablespoons and use olive oil instead of the melted butter. Add to the yeast mixture 4 cloves garlic, minced; 1 teaspoon dried basil, crushed; 1 teaspoon dried rosemary, crushed; and 1 teaspoon dried thyme, crushed. For spiral loaves, divide dough into three portions. Divide each portion into thirds (nine portions total). Gently roll each third into a 24-inch-long rope. Braid three ropes at a time to make three braids; shape each into a spiral loaf. Let rise as directed in Step 4. Instead of brushing with egg mixture, in a small bowl combine 3 tablespoons butter, melted; 1 teaspoon dried basil, crushed; 1 teaspoon dried rosemary, crushed; and 1 clove garlic, minced. Brush over loaves. Bake as directed in Step 5. Makes 3 loaves (36 slices).

Basic Braid Divide dough into three portions before the 10-minute rest in Step 3. Divide each portion into thirds to make nine pieces; roll each piece into a 24-inch rope; braid three ropes together. Repeat with the remaining braids to make two more loaves. Makes 3 loaves.

Multigrain Rolls

PREP 45 minutes
RISE 1 hour 30 minutes
BAKE 12 minutes at 375°F
MAKES 18 servings

3¾ to 4¼ cups all-purpose flour
2 packages active dry yeast
1½ cups milk
⅓ cup honey
¼ cup butter or margarine
2 teaspoons salt
2 eggs
⅔ cup whole wheat flour
½ cup rye flour
½ cup quick-cooking rolled oats
⅓ cup toasted wheat germ
1 tablespoon cornmeal
 Cornmeal or quick-cooking rolled oats
1 egg, slightly beaten
1 tablespoon water
 Sesame seeds, poppy seeds, chia seeds, cornmeal, or oats

1. In a large mixing bowl stir together 2 cups of the all-purpose flour and the yeast; set aside. In a medium saucepan heat and stir milk, honey, butter, and salt just until warm (120°F to 130°F) and butter is almost melted. Add to flour mixture along with the 2 eggs. Beat with a mixer on medium for 30 seconds, scraping sides of bowl frequently. Beat on high for 3 minutes. Using a wooden spoon, stir in whole wheat and rye flours, the ½ cup oats, the wheat germ, and the 1 tablespoon cornmeal. Stir in as much of the remaining all-purpose flour as you can.
2. Turn dough out onto a lightly floured surface. Knead in enough of the remaining all-purpose flour to make a moderately stiff dough that is smooth and elastic (6 to 8 minutes total). Shape dough into a ball. Place in a greased bowl; turn once to grease surface of dough. Cover; let rise until double (1 to 1½ hours).
3. Punch dough down. Turn dough out onto a lightly floured surface. Divide dough into six portions. Cover; let rest for 10 minutes. Meanwhile, lightly grease two large baking sheets. Lightly sprinkle baking sheets with additional cornmeal or oats.
4. Divide each portion of dough into thirds. Shape each third into a ball by pulling dough and pinching underneath. Flatten and pull each ball to form a 4×2-inch oval. Place on the prepared baking sheets. Using kitchen shears, make three slanted cuts about ¾ inch deep on both long sides of each oval, creating a feathered look. Cover; let rise in a warm place until nearly double in size (30 to 45 minutes).
5. Preheat oven to 375°F. In a small bowl combine the beaten egg with the water. Brush rolls with the egg mixture. Sprinkle rolls with sesame seeds, poppy seeds, chai seeds, or oats. Bake for 12 to 15 minutes or until golden. Cool on wire racks.

PER SERVING 211 cal., 5 g fat (2 g sat. fat), 44 mg chol., 298 mg sodium, 36 g carb., 2 g fiber, 7 g pro.

MULTIGRAIN
ROLLS

POTATO-BACON BATTER
BREAD WITH
CARAMELIZED ONIONS

Potato-Bacon Batter Bread with Caramelized Onions

PREP 30 minutes   RISE 40 minutes
BAKE 45 minutes at 375°F
COOL 10 minutes
MAKES 12 servings

  6 slices bacon, chopped
  ½ cup chopped onion (1 medium)
     Cornmeal
  1 cup warm milk (105°F to 115°F)
  1 package active dry yeast
  ⅓ cup butter, melted
  1 egg
  1 teaspoon salt
  3 cups all-purpose flour
  1 cup mashed potatoes* at room
     temperature

1. In a large skillet cook bacon over medium heat until crisp. Using a slotted spoon, transfer bacon to paper towels to drain. Transfer 2 tablespoons of bacon drippings in skillet to a small bowl; set aside. Discard all but 2 tablespoons of the remaining drippings from skillet.
2. Cook onion in hot drippings in skillet over medium heat about 6 minutes or until dark brown. Remove from heat; set aside.
3. Brush the reserved bacon drippings on the bottom and sides of a 2-quart square or rectangular baking pan. Generously sprinkle bottom and sides with cornmeal; set aside.
4. In a large mixing bowl combine warm milk and yeast; let stand until mixture is foamy. Add butter, egg, salt, and 1 cup of the flour. Beat with a mixer on medium for 2 minutes, scraping sides of bowl occasionally. Using a wooden spoon, stir in the remaining 2 cups flour, the bacon, onion, and mashed potatoes until a soft, sticky batter forms.
5. Transfer batter to the prepared pan. Cover; let rise in a warm place until double in size (about 40 minutes).

6. Preheat oven to 375°F. Bake for 45 to 50 minutes or until bread is golden brown. Cool in pan on a wire rack for 10 minutes. Remove bread from dish. Serve warm or cool completely on wire rack.
PER SERVING *23 cal., 12 g fat (6 g sat. fat), 39 mg chol., 331 mg sodium, 30 g carb., 1 g fiber, 6 g pro.*
*Tip For 1 cup mashed potatoes, cook 2 small peeled and quartered red or russet potatoes (12 ounces total) in lightly salted boiling water for 15 to 20 minutes or until very tender; drain well. Mash potatoes with a mixer or potato masher. Or use leftover or refrigerated mashed potatoes.

Smoked Gouda and Ale Loaf

PREP 35 minutes   CHILL overnight
STAND 30 minutes   RISE 1 hour
BAKE 25 minutes at 400°F
MAKES 12 servings

  ¾ cup warm water (105°F to 115°F)
  1 package active dry yeast
  ½ cup ale
  ¼ cup stone ground mustard
  2 tablespoons sugar
  2 tablespoons butter
  1 teaspoon garlic salt
2½ cups all-purpose flour
  ½ cup toasted almonds, ground
  ½ cup shredded smoked Gouda
     cheese (2 ounces)
  ¼ cup crumbled, cooked applewood-
     smoked bacon or regular bacon
  2 teaspoons caraway seeds, toasted
     (see tip, page 19)
     Nonstick cooking spray or olive oil
     Stone ground mustard (optional)

1. In a large bowl stir together the warm water and yeast; let stand about 5 minutes or until yeast is dissolved. Meanwhile, in a small saucepan heat and stir ale, ¼ cup mustard, sugar, butter, and garlic salt just until warm (120°F to 130°F) and butter is almost melted. Stir ale mixture into yeast mixture until combined. Stir in flour, almonds, cheese, bacon, and caraway seeds (dough will be sticky). Lightly coat a medium bowl with cooking spray; transfer dough to the greased

bowl. Lightly coat a sheet of plastic wrap with cooking spray; cover bowl with the greased plastic wrap and chill overnight.
2. Using a dough scraper or spatula, carefully loosen dough from bowl and turn out onto a floured surface. Cover with the greased plastic wrap and let stand for 30 minutes.
3. Grease an 8×8×2-inch baking pan. Press dough into the prepared baking pan. Cover and let rise in a warm place until nearly double in size (about 1 hour).
4. Preheat oven to 400°F. Bake for 25 to 30 minutes or until golden. Remove from pan and cool on a wire rack. If desired, serve with additional mustard. Store in the refrigerator.
PER SERVING *184 cal., 6 g fat (3 g sat. fat), 12 mg chol., 338 mg sodium, 24 g carb., 1 g fiber, 6 g pro.*

SMOKED GOUDA AND ALE LOAF

Spicy Breadsticks with Bacon

PREP **25 minutes**
RISE **1 hour 30 minutes**
BAKE **10 minutes at 425°F**
MAKES **48 servings**

2½ to 3 cups all-purpose flour
  1 package active dry yeast
1¼ cups fat-free milk
  2 tablespoons canola oil
  2 tablespoons honey
  1 teaspoon salt
  ½ cup refrigerated or frozen egg product, thawed
  ¾ cup whole wheat flour
  6 slices turkey bacon, crisp-cooked and finely chopped
  1 tablespoon water
  1 teaspoon crushed red pepper

1. In a large mixing bowl combine 1½ cups of the all-purpose flour and the yeast; set aside. In a small saucepan heat and stir milk, oil, honey, and salt over medium heat until warm (120°F to 130°F). Add to flour mixture along with ¼ cup of the egg. Beat with a mixer on low for 30 seconds, scraping sides of bowl constantly. Beat on high for 3 minutes. Using a wooden spoon, stir in the whole wheat flour, bacon, and as much of the remaining all-purpose flour as you can.
2. Turn dough out onto a lightly floured surface. Knead in enough of the remaining all-purpose flour to make a soft dough that is smooth and elastic

(3 to 5 minutes total). Shape dough into a ball. Place in a lightly greased bowl, turning once to grease surface of dough. Cover and let rise in a warm place until double in size (about 1 hour).
3. Punch dough down. Turn dough out onto a lightly floured surface; cover and let rest for 10 minutes. Meanwhile, line two large baking sheets with foil; grease foil and set aside.
4. On the lightly floured surface, roll dough into a 12×10-inch rectangle. Cut rectangle lengthwise in half. Cut each rectangle crosswise into twenty-four ½-inch-wide strips that are 5 inches long. (You should have 48 strips.) Twist each dough strip a few times, if desired. Space strips 1 inch apart on prepared baking sheets. Cover and let rise in a warm place for 30 minutes or until nearly double in size.
5. Preheat oven to 425°F. In a small bowl combine remaining ¼ cup egg and the 1 tablespoon water. Lightly beat with a fork. Brush lightly over breadsticks. Sprinkle with the crushed red pepper.
6. Bake breadsticks, one pan at a time, for 10 minutes or until breadsticks are lightly browned. Transfer breadsticks to wire racks and cool slightly.
PER SERVING *48 cal., 1 g fat (0 g sat. fat), 1 mg chol., 88 mg sodium, 8 g carb., 0 g fiber, 2 g pro.*

Brandied Brioche

PREP **1 hour**
RISE **2 hours 45 minutes**
CHILL **2 hours**
BAKE **10 minutes at 375°F**
MAKES **12 servings**

  ⅓ cup brandy
  ¾ cup dried currants or snipped dried cherries
  1 package active dry yeast
  ¼ cup warm water (105°F to 115°F)
  ⅔ cup butter, softened
  3 tablespoons granulated sugar
  2 tablespoons packed brown sugar
  ½ teaspoon salt
  3 cups all-purpose flour
  ¼ cup nonfat dry milk powder
  4 eggs
  1 teaspoon vanilla
  1 tablespoon water
  1 Recipe Brandied Icing (optional)

1. In a saucepan bring brandy to boiling over medium heat; remove from heat. Stir in currants. Cover and let stand for 15 minutes; drain, reserving brandy. Set currants and brandy aside.
2. Meanwhile, in a small bowl dissolve yeast in ¼ cup warm water. Let stand for 5 to 10 minutes to soften. In a large mixing bowl beat butter, granulated sugar, brown sugar, and salt with a mixer on medium to high until light and fluffy. Beat in 1 cup of the flour and the milk powder until combined.
3. Separate one of the eggs (chill egg white until needed). Add the egg yolk, the remaining 3 whole eggs, the reserved currants, 1 tablespoon of the reserved brandy, softened yeast, and vanilla to butter mixture; beat well. Stir in the remaining 2 cups flour until smooth. Transfer dough to a greased bowl. Cover and let rise in a warm place until double in size (about 2 hours). Chill for 2 hours.
4. Grease 12 individual brioche pans or 2½-inch muffin cups; set aside. Stir down dough. Turn dough out onto a lightly floured surface. Divide dough into four portions; set one portion aside. Divide each of the remaining three portions into four pieces (12 pieces total).
5. To shape rolls, form each piece into a ball by pulling dough and pinching underneath. Place in the prepared pans. Divide the reserved portion into 12 pieces; form into small balls. Using a floured finger, make an indention in each large ball. Press a small ball into each indention. Cover and let rise in a warm place until nearly double in size (45 to 60 minutes).
6. Preheat oven to 375°F. In a small bowl combine the reserved egg white and 1 tablespoon water; brush over rolls. Bake for 10 to 12 minutes or until golden. Immediately remove rolls from pans; cool on a wire rack. If desired, drizzle with Brandied Icing.
PER SERVING *358 cal., 13 g fat (7 g sat. fat), 91 mg chol., 228 mg sodium, 51 g carb., 2 g fiber, 7 g pro.*
Brandied Icing In a bowl stir together 1⅓ cup powdered sugar, 2 teaspoons softened butter, 1 teaspoon brandy, and ½ teaspoon vanilla. Stir in enough milk to reach drizzling consistency.

SPICY BREADSTICKS WITH BACON

BRANDIED
BRIOCHE

CINNAMON ROLL
CHRISTMAS TREE

Cinnamon Roll Christmas Tree

PREP **45 minutes**
RISE **1 hour 15 minutes**
BAKE **30 minutes at 350°F**
COOL **10 minutes**
MAKES **11 servings**

- 4¼ to 4¾ cups all-purpose flour
- 1 package active dry yeast
- 1¾ cups milk
- ½ cup instant mashed potato flakes
- ⅓ cup butter, cut up
- ⅓ cup sugar
- 1 teaspoon salt
- 2 eggs
- ½ cup packed brown sugar
- 1 tablespoon ground cinnamon
- ¼ cup butter, softened
- 1 3-ounce package cream cheese, softened
- 2 tablespoons softened butter
- 2½ cups powdered sugar
- 1 teaspoon vanilla
  Milk or orange juice

1. In a large mixing bowl combine 1½ cups of the all-purpose flour and the yeast; set aside. In a medium saucepan heat and stir milk, potato flakes, the ⅓ cup butter, the sugar, and salt just until warm (120°F to 130°F) and butter is almost melted. Add butter mixture to flour mixture; add eggs. Beat with a mixer on low to medium for 30 seconds, scraping sides of bowl constantly. Beat on high for 3 minutes, scraping sides of bowl occasionally. Using a wooden spoon, stir in as much of the remaining flour as you can.
2. Turn dough out onto a lightly floured surface. Knead in enough of the remaining flour to make a moderately soft dough that is smooth and elastic (3 to 5 minutes total). Shape dough into a ball. Place in a lightly greased bowl, turning once to grease surface of dough. Cover and let rise in a warm place until double in size (45 to 60 minutes).
3. Punch dough down. Turn dough out onto a lightly floured surface. Cover and let rest for 10 minutes. Meanwhile, for filling, in a bowl stir together the brown sugar and cinnamon; set aside.

4. Roll dough into an 18×12-inch rectangle. Spread the ¼ cup butter on dough and sprinkle with filling, leaving about 1 inch unfilled along one long side. Roll up rectangle, starting from the filled long side; pinch dough to seal seams. Slice into 11 equal pieces.
5. Line an extra-large baking sheet with parchment paper. Place one roll at the bottom of prepared baking sheet for trunk. Arrange a row of four, three, two, then one roll to shape a tree, snuggling rolls closely. Cover and let rise in a warm place until nearly double in size (about 30 minutes).
6. Preheat oven to 350°F. Place tree on middle oven rack. Line a baking sheet with foil; place on bottom rack to catch any drips. Bake for 30 to 35 minutes or until golden, covering edges with foil if necessary to prevent overbrowning. Cool for 10 minutes before icing.
7. For the icing, in a small bowl combine cream cheese, the 2 tablespoons butter, powdered sugar, vanilla, and enough milk or orange juice to reach desired consistency. Drizzle tree with icing.
PER SERVING *399 cal., 11 g fat (6 g sat. fat), 58 mg chol., 313 mg sodium, 68 g carb., 2 g fiber, 8 g pro.*

Fig-Pistachio Cranberry Loaf

PREP **30 minutes**
BAKE **1 hour 5 minutes at 350°F**
COOL **10 minutes** STAND **overnight**
MAKES **14 servings**

- 2 cups all-purpose flour
- 1 cup sugar
- 2 teaspoons baking powder
- ½ teaspoon salt
- 1 teaspoon finely shredded orange peel
- 2 eggs, lightly beaten
- ½ cup milk
- ½ cup butter, melted
- ¾ cup coarsely chopped cranberries
- ¾ cup chopped pistachio nuts
- ½ cup chopped dried figs

1. Preheat oven to 350°F. Grease the bottom and ½ inch up the sides of an 8×4×2-inch loaf pan; set aside. In a large bowl stir together flour, sugar, baking powder, and salt. Stir in orange peel. Make a well in the center of flour mixture; set aside.
2. In a medium bowl combine eggs, milk, and melted butter. Add egg mixture all at once to flour mixture. Stir just until moistened (batter should be lumpy). Fold in cranberries, pistachios, and figs. Spoon batter into the prepared loaf pan, spreading evenly.
3. Bake for 65 to 70 minutes or until a wooden toothpick inserted near the center comes out clean. If necessary to prevent overbrowning, cover loosely with foil during the last 15 minutes of baking.
4. Cool in pan on a wire rack for 10 minutes. Remove from pan. Cool completely on wire rack. Wrap and store overnight before slicing.
PER SERVING *196 cal., 8 g fat (5 g sat. fat), 48 mg chol., 178 mg sodium, 29 g carb., 1 g fiber, 3 g pro.*

FIG-PISTACHIO CRANBERRY LOAF

APRICOT-ANISE NUT BREAD

Apricot-Anise Nut Bread

PREP 30 minutes
BAKE 50 minutes at 350°F
COOL 10 minutes STAND overnight
MAKES 14 servings

    2 cups all-purpose flour
    1 cup granulated sugar
    1 tablespoon baking powder
    ½ teaspoon salt
    ½ teaspoon anise seeds, crushed
    1 egg, lightly beaten
    ¾ cup milk
    ½ cup apricot nectar
    ¼ cup vegetable oil
    1 cup mixed nuts, chopped
    ¾ cup snipped dried apricots
    1 cup powdered sugar
    1 tablespoon whipping cream,
       light cream, or milk
    1 teaspoon vanilla
       Whipping cream, light cream,
       or milk

1. Preheat oven to 350°F. Grease the bottom and ½ inch up the sides of an 8×4×2-inch loaf pan; set aside. In a large bowl stir together flour, granulated sugar, baking powder, salt, and anise seeds. Make a well in the center of flour mixture; set aside.
2. In a medium bowl combine egg, ¾ cup milk, apricot nectar, and oil. Add egg mixture all at once to flour mixture. Stir just until moistened (batter should be lumpy). Fold in nuts and dried apricots. Spoon batter into the prepared loaf pan, spreading evenly.
3. Bake for 50 to 55 minutes or until a wooden toothpick inserted near the center comes out clean. Cool in pan on a wire rack for 10 minutes. Remove from pan. Cool completely on wire rack. Wrap and store overnight.
4. For frosting, in a small bowl stir together powdered sugar, 1 tablespoon whipping cream, and vanilla. Stir in enough additional whipping cream to reach drizzling consistency. Drizzle loaf with frosting before slicing.
PER SERVING *293 cal., 11 g fat (2 g sat. fat), 17 mg chol., 229 mg sodium, 45 g carb., 2 g fiber, 5 g pro.*

Triple-Chocolate Bread

PREP 25 minutes
BAKE 45 minutes at 350°F
COOL 10 minutes STAND overnight
MAKES 14 servings

    2 cups all-purpose flour
    1 cup sugar
    3 tablespoons unsweetened cocoa
       powder
    1 tablespoon baking powder
    ½ teaspoon salt
    1 egg, lightly beaten
  1¼ cups milk
    ½ cup vegetable oil
    ⅓ cup white baking pieces
    ⅓ cup dark chocolate pieces
    ⅓ cup milk chocolate pieces
       Sweetened whipped cream
       (optional)
       Dark chocolate pieces or
       milk chocolate pieces, melted
       (optional)

1. Preheat oven to 350°F. Grease the bottom and ½ inch up the sides of a 9×5×3-inch loaf pan. Line bottom of pan with waxed paper or parchment paper; grease paper. Set pan aside. In a large bowl stir together flour, sugar, cocoa powder, baking powder, and salt. Make a well in the center of flour mixture; set aside.
2. In a medium bowl combine egg, milk, and oil. Add egg mixture all at once to flour mixture. Stir just until moistened (batter should be lumpy). Fold in white baking pieces, ⅓ cup dark chocolate pieces, and ⅓ cup milk chocolate pieces. Spoon batter into the prepared loaf pan, spreading evenly.
3. Bake for 45 to 55 minutes or until a wooden toothpick inserted in the center comes out clean. Cool in pan on a wire rack for 10 minutes. Remove from pan; peel off paper. Cool completely on wire rack. Wrap and store overnight before slicing.
4. If desired, top each serving with sweetened whipped cream and drizzle with melted chocolate.
PER SERVING *268 cal., 13 g fat (3 g sat. fat), 17 mg chol., 177 mg sodium, 38 g carb., 2 g fiber, 4 g pro.*

TRIPLE-CHOCOLATE
BREAD

Blueberry-Lemon Loaf

PREP 30 minutes
BAKE 1 hour at 350°F
COOL 10 minutes STAND overnight
MAKES 14 servings

- 2 cups all-purpose flour
- 1 cup sugar
- 2 teaspoons baking powder
- ½ teaspoon salt
- 1 teaspoon finely shredded lemon peel
- 2 eggs, lightly beaten
- ½ cup milk
- ½ cup butter, melted
- ¾ cup blueberries

1. Preheat oven to 350°F. Grease the bottom and ½ inch up the sides of an 8×4×2-inch loaf pan. In a bowl stir together flour, sugar, baking powder, and salt. Stir in lemon peel. Make a well in the center of flour mixture.
2. In a medium bowl combine eggs, milk, and melted butter. Add egg mixture all at once to flour mixture. Stir just until moistened (batter should be lumpy). Fold in blueberries. Spoon batter into the prepared loaf pan, spreading evenly.
3. Bake for 60 to 70 minutes or until a wooden toothpick inserted near the center comes out clean. If necessary to prevent overbrowning, cover loosely with foil during the last 15 minutes of baking.
4. Cool in pan on a wire rack for 10 minutes. Remove from pan. Cool completely on wire rack. Wrap and store overnight before slicing.

PER SERVING 198 cal., 8 g fat (5 g sat. fat), 45 mg chol., 225 mg sodium, 30 g carb., 1 g fiber, 3 g pro.

Honey-Almond Breakfast Biscuits with Mango-Apricot Spread

PREP 25 minutes
BAKE 12 minutes at 400°F
MAKES 25 servings

- 2⅔ cups all-purpose flour
- ⅔ cup whole wheat pastry flour
- ¼ cup almond flour
- ¼ cup finely chopped, toasted almonds (see tip, page 19)
- 1 tablespoon baking powder
- ¼ teaspoon salt
- ⅓ cup cold light butter, cut up
- ⅔ cup fat-free milk
- ½ cup refrigerated or frozen egg product, thawed, or 2 eggs, lightly beaten
- ¼ cup honey
- ½ cup chopped refrigerated mango slices
- ⅓ cup low-sugar apricot preserves
- ⅛ teaspoon ground cardamom

1. Preheat oven to 400°F. In a large bowl combine flours, almonds, baking powder, and salt. Using a pastry blender, cut in butter until mixture resembles coarse crumbs. Make a well in center of the flour mixture; set aside.
2. In a bowl combine milk, eggs, and honey. Add all at once to flour. Using a fork, stir just until moistened.
3. Turn dough out onto a floured surface. Knead by folding and gently pressing dough for 6 to 8 strokes or until nearly smooth. Pat or lightly roll dough to ¾-inch thickness. Using a 2-inch fluted round cutter, cut out biscuits. Reroll scraps as needed; avoid overworking dough when rerolling to prevent tough biscuits. Place biscuits 2 inches apart on an extra-large greased baking sheet.
4. Bake for 12 to 15 minutes or until golden. Cool slightly on a wire rack.
5. For spread, place mango in a small microwave-safe bowl. Cover with vented plastic wrap. Cook on 100% power for 1 to 1½ minutes or until mango is tender, stirring once. Mash with a fork. Stir in apricot preserves and cardamom. Serve with warm biscuits.

PER SERVING 99 cal., 2 g fat (1 g sat. fat), 3 mg chol., 116 mg sodium, 17 g carb., 1 g fiber, 3 g pro.

BLUEBERRY-LEMON LOAF

HONEY-ALMOND
BREAKFAST BISCUITS
WITH MANGO-APRICOT
SPREAD

MANCHEGO AND
BRANDIED CHERRY
SCONES

Manchego and Brandied Cherry Scones

PREP 25 minutes
STAND 15 minutes
CHILL 30 minutes
BAKE 20 minutes at 375°F
MAKES 8 servings

- ½ cup snipped dried cherries
- ¼ cup brandy or apple juice
- 1¾ cups all-purpose flour
- ½ cup finely shredded Manchego or Asiago cheese (2 ounces)
- 1 tablespoon baking powder
- 1 tablespoon sugar
- ¼ teaspoon salt
- ¼ cup cold butter, cut up
- ⅔ cup whipping cream
- 1 egg
- 1 tablespoon water
- ½ teaspoon very finely snipped fresh rosemary
- ¼ teaspoon coarse salt or kosher salt
- ¼ teaspoon coarsely ground black pepper

1. Line a baking sheet with parchment paper; set aside. In a small saucepan combine cherries and brandy over medium heat just until warm. Remove from heat. Cover and let stand for 15 minutes; drain.
2. In a food processor* combine flour, ¼ cup of the cheese, the baking powder, sugar, and ¼ teaspoon salt. Cover and pulse with several on/off turns to combine. Sprinkle butter pieces over flour mixture. Cover and pulse with several on/off turns until mixture resembles coarse crumbs. Add drained cherries; cover and pulse with several on/off turns to combine. With the motor running, slowly add whipping cream through the feed tube, processing just until combined.
3. Turn dough out onto a lightly floured surface. Knead by folding and gently pressing it 10 to 12 strokes or just until it holds together. Pat or lightly roll dough into an 8-inch circle. In a small bowl whisk together egg and the water; brush over dough. In a small bowl stir together the remaining ¼ cup cheese, the rosemary, coarse salt, and pepper. Sprinkle over dough. Using a pizza cutter or sharp floured knife, cut dough into eight wedges. Place wedges 2 inches apart on the prepared baking sheet. Cover and chill for 30 minutes.
4. Preheat oven to 375°F. Bake about 20 minutes or until golden. Serve warm.

PER SERVING 329 cal., 18 g fat (11 g sat. fat), 76 mg chol., 504 mg sodium, 31 g carb., 1 g fiber, 7 g pro.

*Tip If you don't have a food processor, combine the flour mixture in a large bowl. Using a pastry blender, cut in butter until mixture resembles coarse crumbs. Make a well in the center of the flour mixture. Add drained cherries and whipping cream all at once. Using a fork, stir until dough is moistened. Continue as directed in Step 4.

Flaky Biscuits

PREP 15 minutes
BAKE 10 minutes at 450°F
MAKES 12 servings

- 3 cups all-purpose flour
- 1 tablespoon baking powder*
- 1 tablespoon sugar
- 1 teaspoon salt
- ¾ teaspoon cream of tartar*
- ¾ cup butter or ½ cup butter and ¼ cup shortening
- 1 cup milk

1. Preheat oven to 450°F. In a large bowl combine flour, baking powder, sugar, salt, and cream of tartar. Using a pastry blender, cut in butter until mixture resembles coarse crumbs. Make a well in the center of the flour mixture. Add milk all at once. Using a fork, stir just until moistened.
2. Turn dough out onto a lightly floured surface. Knead by folding and gently pressing dough four to six strokes or just until it holds together. Pat or lightly roll dough to ¾-inches thick. Cut dough with a floured biscuit cutter, dipping cutter in flour between cuts, and rerolling scraps as needed.
3. Place biscuits 1 inch apart on an ungreased baking sheet. Bake for 10 to 14 minutes or until golden. Remove biscuits from baking sheet and serve warm.

PER SERVING 269 cal., 15 g fat (9 g sat. fat), 42 mg chol., 486 mg sodium, 26 g carb., 1 g fiber, 6 g pro.

*Tip If baking powder or cream of tartar appears lumpy, sift through a fine-mesh sieve before using.

Pimiento Corn Muffins

PREP 20 minutes
BAKE 18 minutes at 400°F
COOL 5 minutes MAKES 8 servings

- 1 egg, lightly beaten
- 1 8.5-ounce package corn muffin mix
- 1 cup frozen whole kernel corn
- ⅓ cup milk
- 2 tablespoons snipped fresh cilantro
- 1 tablespoon diced pimiento
- ½ to 1 teaspoon ground cumin

1. Preheat oven to 400°F. Line eight 2½-inch muffin cups with paper bake cups; set aside.
2. In a medium bowl combine egg, muffin mix, corn, milk, cilantro, pimiento, and cumin. Stir just until moistened. Spoon ¼ cup batter into each prepared muffin cup.
3. Bake for 18 minutes or until muffin tops are golden. Cool in muffin cups on a wire rack for 5 minutes. Remove from muffin cups; serve warm.

PER SERVING 153 cal., 4 g fat (0 g sat. fat), 24 mg chol., 225 mg sodium, 26 g carb., 0 g fiber, 4 g pro.

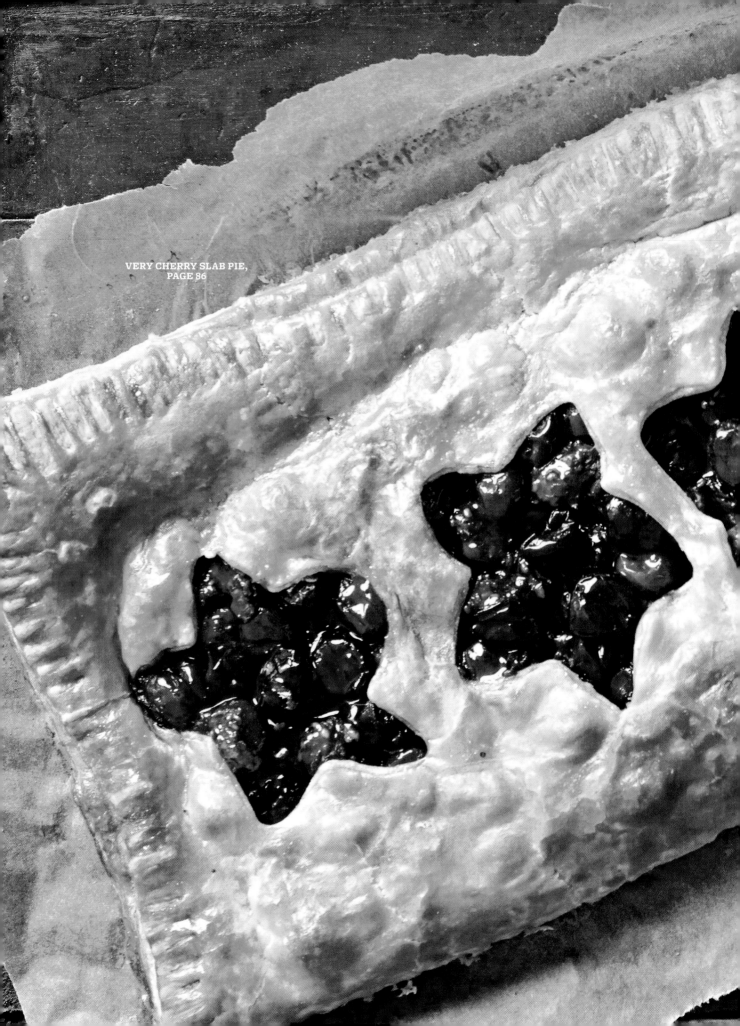

VERY CHERRY SLAB PIE,
PAGE 86

Some Kind of Wonderful

IF THERE IS ONE TIME of the year to indulge in decadent desserts, this is it. These fabulous pies, tarts, cakes, pastries, and fruit cobblers are sweet reminders that this season is rich with out-of-the-ordinary moments we remember all year long.

BLOOD ORANGE
POUND CAKE

Blood Orange Pound Cake

PREP 30 minutes STAND 30 minutes
BAKE 45 minutes at 350°F
COOL 1 hour MAKES 12 servings

1¼ cups butter
3 eggs
2¼ cups all-purpose flour
¾ teaspoon baking powder
½ teaspoon baking soda
½ teaspoon salt
⅓ cup milk
1 tablespoon + 2 teaspoons finely shredded blood orange peel
2 tablespoons blood orange juice
1½ cups granulated sugar
2 teaspoons vanilla
½ cup powdered sugar
½ cup blood orange juice
2 tablespoons butter, melted
2 tablespoons dark rum
1 teaspoon cornstarch
1 cup whipping cream
3 to 4 blood oranges, thinly sliced

1. Allow the 1¼ cups butter and eggs to stand at room temperature for 30 minutes. Meanwhile, grease and flour a 10-inch tube pan; set aside. In a medium bowl stir together flour, baking powder, baking soda, and salt. In a small bowl combine milk, 1 tablespoon of the orange peel, and the 2 tablespoons orange juice. Set aside.
2. Preheat oven to 350°F. In a large mixing bowl beat the room-temperature butter with a mixer on medium to high for 30 seconds. Add granulated sugar, beating until combined. Add eggs, one at a time, beating well after each addition. Stir in vanilla. Alternately add flour mixture and milk mixture to butter mixture, beating on low after each addition just until combined.
3. Pour batter into the prepared pan, spreading evenly. Bake for 45 minutes or until a wooden toothpick inserted near the center comes out clean. Cool in pan on a wire rack for 10 minutes. Remove cake from pan and place on wire rack set over waxed paper. Using a long wooden skewer, poke several holes all over cake.
4. For sauce, in a small saucepan stir together powdered sugar, ½ cup

ALMOND BRICKLE
RING CAKE

orange juice, 2 tablespoons melted butter, rum, and cornstarch. Cook and stir over medium heat until thickened and bubbly. Cook and stir for 2 minutes more. Brush ¼ cup of the sauce over warm cake. Cool cake completely. Cover the remaining sauce; set aside.
5. Before serving, in a chilled medium mixing bowl beat whipping cream on medium until soft peaks form (tips curl). Fold in the remaining 2 teaspoons orange peel.
6. Spoon some of the remaining sauce over cake. Top with orange slices and the remaining sauce. Serve cake with whipped cream.
PER SERVING *510 cal., 30 g fat (19 g sat. fat), 130 mg chol., 388 mg sodium, 55 g carb., 2 g fiber, 5 g pro.*

Almond Brickle Ring Cake

PREP 15 minutes
BAKE 45 minutes at 350°F
COOL 1 hour MAKES 12 servings

1 package 2-layer-size French vanilla cake mix
1 4-serving-size package vanilla instant pudding and pie filling mix
4 eggs
1 cup water
½ cup butter, softened
1 teaspoon almond extract
¾ cup toffee pieces
1 cup powdered sugar
1 tablespoon milk
¼ teaspoon almond extract
Milk (optional)
Purchased almond brittle, coarsely crushed, or toffee pieces

1. Preheat oven to 350°F. Grease and flour a 10-inch fluted tube pan; set aside.
2. In a large mixing bowl combine cake mix, pudding mix, eggs, the water, butter, and 1 teaspoon almond extract. Beat with a mixer on medium for 2 minutes. Fold in the ¾ cup toffee pieces. Pour batter into the prepared pan, spreading evenly.
3. Bake for 45 to 50 minutes or until a wooden toothpick inserted near the center comes out clean. Cool in pan on a wire rack for 15 minutes. Remove cake from pan; cool completely on wire rack.
4. For the glaze, in a small bowl combine powdered sugar, 1 tablespoon milk, and ¼ teaspoon almond extract. If necessary, stir in enough additional milk, 1 teaspoon at a time, to reach drizzling consistency. Drizzle glaze over cake. Immediately sprinkle with crushed almond brittle.
PER SERVING *427 cal., 18 g fat (10 g sat. fat), 96 mg chol., 573 mg sodium, 61 g carb., 0 g fiber, 4 g pro.*

Gingered Fruit Cake

PREP **25 minutes**
BAKE **40 minutes at 350°F**
COOL **10 minutes**
MAKES **10 servings**

- ¾ cup pecan halves, toasted (see tip, page 19)
- 2 cups all-purpose flour
- 1¼ cups sugar
- 1 tablespoon baking powder
- ½ teaspoon salt
- ½ cup milk
- ½ cup butter, softened
- 2 eggs
- 1 cup dried apples, chopped
- ⅔ cup dried apricots, chopped
- 2 tablespoons grated fresh ginger
- 4 to 5 slices fresh red apple
- 5 to 6 dried apricot halves (not unsulfured)
- 2 tablespoons pecan halves
- ¼ cup butter
- 1 tablespoon honey
- 1 tablespoon bourbon or rum

GINGERED
FRUIT CAKE

1. Preheat oven to 350°F. Generously grease and lightly flour a 9-inch springform pan; set aside.
2. Place ½ cup of the toasted pecans in a food processor; cover and process until finely ground. In a large mixing bowl combine ground pecans, flour, sugar, baking powder, and salt. Add milk, ½ cup butter, and eggs. Beat with a mixer on low until combined. Beat on medium for 1 minute (batter will be thick). Fold in chopped dried apples, chopped dried apricots, and ginger. Transfer to prepared pan; spread evenly. Arrange fresh apple slices, dried apricot halves, and the remaining pecan halves over batter.
3. Bake for 40 minutes or until a wooden toothpick inserted near center comes out clean. Cool in pan on wire rack 10 minutes. Remove sides of pan. Cool completely on a wire rack. Remove bottom of pan.
4. To serve, in a small saucepan melt ¼ cup butter; whisk in honey and bourbon. Brush some of the sauce over cake before slicing. Serve with remaining sauce.
PER SERVING *451 cal., 20 g fat (10 g sat. fat), 75 mg chol., 460 mg sodium, 64 g carb., 3 g fiber, 6 g pro.*

Champagne Cake

PREP **40 minutes**
STAND **30 minutes**
BAKE **40 minutes at 350°F**
COOL **1 hour** MAKES **9 servings**

- ½ cup butter
- 4 egg whites
- 2 cups all-purpose flour
- 2¼ teaspoons baking powder
- ¾ teaspoon salt
- 1 cup sugar
- 1½ teaspoons vanilla
- 1 cup champagne
- 1 Recipe Champagne Butter Frosting

1. Allow butter and egg whites to stand at room temperature for 30 minutes. Meanwhile, grease an 8×8×2-inch or 9×9×2-inch baking pan. Line bottom of pan with parchment paper. Grease paper and lightly flour pan; set aside. In a medium bowl stir together flour, baking powder, and salt; set aside.
2. Preheat oven to 350°F. In a large mixing bowl beat butter with a mixer on medium to high for 30 seconds. Add sugar and vanilla. Beat on medium about 3 minutes or until light and fluffy. Alternately add flour mixture and champagne to butter mixture, beating on low after each addition just until combined.
3. Wash beaters thoroughly. In a medium mixing bowl beat egg whites on with a mixer on high until stiff peaks form (tips stand straight). Fold beaten egg whites into cake batter. Pour batter into the prepared pan.
4. Bake for 40 to 45 minutes or until a wooden toothpick inserted in the center comes out clean. Cool in pan on a wire rack for 10 minutes. Remove cake from pan; remove parchment paper. Cool completely on wire rack. Frost top and sides of cake with Champagne Butter Frosting.
Champagne Butter Frosting In a large mixing bowl beat 6 tablespoons butter with a mixer on medium to high for 30 seconds. Gradually add 1 cup powdered sugar, beating well. Slowly beat in 4 to 5 tablespoons champagne, sparkling wine, or milk, and 1 teaspoon vanilla. Gradually beat in 3 cups powdered sugar. Beat in enough additional champagne until frosting reaches spreading consistency.
PER SERVING *685 cal., 23 g fat (15 g sat. fat), 47 mg chol., 491 mg sodium, 111 g carb., 1 g fiber, 5 g pro.*
Strawberry Champagne Cake
Thaw one 10-ounce package frozen strawberries in syrup. Drain well, discarding syrup. Snip strawberries into small pieces with kitchen scissors. Prepare Champagne Cake as directed, except stir strawberries and, if desired, 2 to 3 drops red food coloring into batter before folding in beaten egg whites. Pour batter into a 9×9×2-inch baking pan. Bake for 50 minutes or until a wooden toothpick inserted in the center comes out clean. Continue as directed.

STRAWBERRY
CHAMPAGNE CAKE

Raspberry-Filled Cake Roll

PREP 1 hour CHILL 10 hours
BAKE 12 minutes at 375°F
COOL 1 hour MAKES 10 servings

  1 recipe Raspberry Filling
  4 eggs
  ½ cup all-purpose flour
  1 teaspoon baking powder
  ½ teaspoon vanilla
  ⅓ cup granulated sugar
  ½ cup granulated sugar
     Powdered sugar

1. Prepare Raspberry Filling; chill as directed.

2. Separate eggs. Allow egg whites and yolks to stand at room temperature for 30 minutes. Meanwhile, grease a 15×10×1-inch baking pan. Line bottom of pan with waxed paper or parchment paper; grease paper. Set pan aside.

3. Preheat oven to 375°F. In a small bowl stir together flour and baking powder; set aside. In a medium mixing bowl beat egg yolks and vanilla with a mixer on high about 5 minutes or until thick and lemon color. Gradually add ⅓ cup granulated sugar, beating on high until sugar is almost dissolved.

4. Thoroughly wash beaters. In a large mixing bowl beat egg whites on medium until soft peaks form (tips curl). Gradually add ½ cup granulated sugar, beating until stiff peaks form (tips stand straight). Fold egg yolk mixture into beaten egg whites. Sprinkle flour mixture over egg mixture; fold in gently just until combined. Spread batter evenly in the prepared baking pan.

5. Bake for 12 to 15 minutes or until cake springs back when lightly touched. Immediately loosen edges of cake from pan and turn cake out onto a clean kitchen towel sprinkled with powdered sugar. Remove waxed paper. Roll towel and cake into a spiral, starting from a short side of the cake. Cool on a wire rack.

6. Unroll cake; remove towel. Spread cake with Raspberry Filling to within 1 inch of the edges. Roll up cake; trim ends. Cover and chill up to 6 hours. Before serving, sprinkle with additional powdered sugar. Serve with reserved ½ cup strained raspberries.

PER SERVING *229 cal., 8 g fat (4 g sat. fat), 147 mg chol., 91 mg sodium, 35 g carb., 1 g fiber, 5 g pro.*

Raspberry Filling Place 1½ cups fresh or thawed frozen raspberries in a blender or food processor. Cover and blend or process until pureed. Strain raspberries through a fine-mesh sieve (should have about ¾ cup); discard seeds. Remove about ½ cup of the strained raspberries; cover and chill until ready to serve. In a medium-size heavy saucepan stir together ⅓ cup sugar and 2 tablespoons cornstarch. Gradually stir in the remaining ¼ cup strained raspberries, ½ cup whipping cream, and ½ cup milk. Cook and stir over medium heat until thickened and bubbly. Cook and stir for 1 minute more. Gradually stir about half the hot mixture into two lightly beaten egg yolks. Return egg yolk mixture to saucepan. Bring to a gentle boil; reduce heat. Cook and stir for 2 minutes. Pour into a medium bowl; stir in 1 tablespoon raspberry liqueur (if desired) and ½ teaspoon vanilla. Tint with 10 to 12 drops red food coloring. Place bowl of filling in a larger bowl of ice water; chill for 5 minutes, stirring occasionally. Cover surface with plastic wrap. Chill about 4 hours or until cold.

Rum Babas

PREP 1 hour RISE 1 hour 20 minutes
BAKE 15 minutes at 350°F
MAKES 8 servings

    2 cups all-purpose flour
    1 package active dry yeast
    ⅓ cup milk
    1 tablespoon sugar
    ½ teaspoon salt
    4 eggs
    ½ cup butter
    ¾ cup raisins and/or golden raisins
    1 teaspoon finely shredded orange
       peel
  1½ cups water
    ¾ cup sugar
    ⅓ cup rum or orange juice
    ½ cup apricot preserves
    1 tablespoon water

1. In a large mixing bowl stir together 1½ cups of the flour and the yeast; set aside. In a small saucepan heat and stir milk, 1 tablespoon sugar, and salt just until warm (120°F to 130°F).
2. Add milk mixture to flour mixture. Add eggs. Beat with a mixer on low to medium for 30 seconds, scraping sides of the bowl constantly. Beat on high for 3 minutes. Using a wooden spoon, stir in the remaining flour (batter will be very sticky and soft). Cut butter into small pieces; place on top of batter. Cover and let rise in a warm place until double in size (about 1 hour).
3. Grease eight ½-cup popover cups, twelve ½-cup baba molds, or twelve 2½-inch muffin cups; set aside.
4. Stir butter, raisins, and orange peel into batter. Divide batter among prepared cups or molds, filling each one-half to two-thirds full. Cover and let rise in a warm place until batter nearly fills cups or molds (20 to 30 minutes). (Or cover and chill overnight. Let stand at room temperature for 20 minutes before baking.)
5. Preheat oven to 350°F. Bake for 15 to 20 minutes or until golden. Remove babas from cups or molds and cool on wire racks set over waxed paper.
6. For rum syrup, in a small heavy saucepan stir together 1½ cups water and ¾ cup sugar. Stir over medium heat until sugar is dissolved. Bring to boiling. Boil, without stirring, for 5 minutes; cool slightly. Stir in rum.
7. Prick babas all over with the tines of a fork. Holding babas upside down, dip two or three times in the rum syrup to moisten. Return to wire racks. Spoon any remaining syrup over babas.
8. For glaze, snip any large pieces of fruit in the preserves. In a small saucepan combine preserves and 1 tablespoon water. Stir over low heat until preserves are melted. Brush glaze over babas.

PER SERVING *457 cal., 15 g fat (8 g sat. fat), 124 mg chol., 298 mg sodium, 70 g carb., 2 g fiber, 8 g pro.*

Caramel-Orange Profiteroles

PREP 50 minutes COOL 10 minutes
BAKE 25 minutes at 400°F
MAKES 24 servings

    ½ 8-ounce carton mascarpone
       cheese
    ½ cup whipping cream
    2 tablespoons powdered sugar
    2 tablespoons orange marmalade
    ¼ teaspoon vanilla
    ½ cup water
    ¼ cup butter
       Dash salt
    ½ cup all-purpose flour
    2 eggs
    1 cup good-quality caramel sauce
       (with butter in the ingredient list)
    2 tablespoons orange liqueur
    ¼ cup chopped toasted pecans
       (see tip, page 19) (optional)

1. For filling, in a medium mixing bowl beat mascarpone, whipping cream, powdered sugar, marmalade, and vanilla with a mixer on medium to high just until stiff peaks form (tips stand straight), scraping sides of bowl occasionally. Cover and chill up to 24 hours.
2. Preheat oven to 400°F. Grease an extra-large baking sheet; set aside. In a small saucepan combine the water, butter, and salt. Bring to boiling. Immediately add flour all at once; stir vigorously. Cook and stir until mixture forms a ball. Remove from heat. Cool for 10 minutes. Add eggs, one at a time, beating with a wooden spoon after each addition until smooth.
3. Spoon dough into a pastry bag fitted with a ½-inch open star tip. Pipe dough onto prepared baking sheet, making a total of 24 puffs. Or drop dough by rounded teaspoons 2 inches apart onto prepared baking sheet. (If you need to use two baking sheets, keep the second pan covered while the first pan bakes.) Bake for 25 minutes. Transfer puffs to wire racks; cool completely.
4. Before serving, in a small saucepan stir caramel sauce over medium heat just until warm. Remove from heat; stir in liqueur. Set aside.
5. To serve, cut tops from puffs; remove soft dough from inside. Spoon filling into bottoms of puffs; replace tops. Spoon caramel sauce onto puffs. If desired, sprinkle with pecans.

PER SERVING *121 cal., 6 g fat (4 g sat. fat), 33 mg chol., 64 mg sodium, 14 g carb., 0 g fiber, 3 g pro.*

RUM BABAS

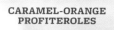
CARAMEL-ORANGE
PROFITEROLES

MAPLE MASCARPONE CHEESECAKE

cheesecake is puffy around the edges and wiggles slightly when gently shaken. Cool in pan on a wire rack for 20 minutes.

4. In a small bowl stir together yogurt, maple syrup, the ½ teaspoon vanilla, and the ⅛ teaspoon salt. Spread yogurt mixture evenly over cheesecake, spreading to within ½ inch of edge. Bake for 10 minutes more. Remove cheesecake from oven; while hot, run a thin metal spatula around the edge of the cheesecake. Cool in pan on a wire rack. Chill for at least 8 hours or up to 5 days before serving.

5. To serve, loosen the edge of the cheesecake from sides of pan; remove sides of t pan. If desired, top cheesecake with Candied Walnuts.

PER SERVING *481 cal., 39 g fat (18 g sat. fat), 132 mg chol., 292 mg sodium, 26 g carb., 1 g fiber, 12 g pro.*

Candied Walnuts Preheat oven to 325°F. Spread 3 cups walnut pieces on a foil-lined baking sheet. Bake for 10 minutes, stirring once. Meanwhile, heat ½ cup sugar in a medium-size heavy skillet over medium-high heat, shaking skillet occasionally to heat sugar evenly. Do not stir. Heat until some of is sugar melted; stir only the melted sugar to keep it from overbrowning. Stir in remaining sugar as it melts. Reduce heat to medium-low; continue to cook until all the sugar is melted and golden. Stir in 2 tablespoons butter until melted and combined. Remove from heat. Stir in the warm walnuts until coated. Return coated walnuts to the baking sheet, spreading evenly. Cool completely and break apart.

Maple Mascarpone Cheesecake

PREP 35 minutes
BAKE 33 minutes at 350°F
COOL 20 minutes CHILL 8 hours
MAKES 12 servings

Butter
1½ cups walnut pieces
¼ cup granulated sugar
¼ cup butter, melted
19 ounces cream cheese, softened
8 ounces mascarpone cheese, softened
⅓ cup granulated sugar
⅓ cup packed light brown sugar
3 eggs
1 teaspoon vanilla
1 teaspoon maple flavoring
¼ teaspoon salt
1 cup plain Greek yogurt
¼ cup pure maple syrup
½ teaspoon vanilla
⅛ teaspoon salt
Candied Walnuts (optional)

1. Preheat oven to 350°F. Butter a 10-inch springform pan; set aside. In a food processor or blender combine the 1½ cups walnut pieces and the ¼ cup granulated sugar; cover and pulse or blend with several on/off turns until fine crumbs form. Add the ¼ cup melted butter; pulse or blend to mix. Press crumb mixture firmly onto the bottom of the prepared springform pan. Bake for 8 to 10 minutes or until crust is firm and lightly browned on the edges. Cool in pan on a wire rack.

2. Meanwhile, in a large mixing bowl combine cream cheese, mascarpone, the ⅓ cup granulated sugar, and the brown sugar. Beat with a mixer on medium-high about 5 minutes or until very light and fluffy. Scrape sides of bowl; beat for 1 minute more. Add eggs, one at a time, beating well after each addition. Stir in the 1 teaspoon vanilla, the maple flavoring, and the ¼ teaspoon salt; mix well.

3. Pour filling into cooled crust. Bake for 25 to 30 minutes or until

Cherry Cobbler with White Chocolate-Almond Biscuits

PREP 35 minutes
BAKE 25 minutes at 375°F
COOL 1 hour MAKES 12 servings

1¾ cups all-purpose flour
¼ cup granulated sugar
4 teaspoons baking powder
½ teaspoon salt
½ cup butter, cut up
12 cups frozen unsweetened pitted tart red cherries (3½ pounds)

2 cups granulated sugar
6 tablespoons cornstarch
2 eggs, lightly beaten
¾ cup milk
1 teaspoon almond extract
½ teaspoon vanilla
8 ounces white baking chocolate with cocoa butter, cut into ½-inch chunks
1 cup slivered almonds, toasted (see tip, page 19) and coarsely chopped
  Pearl or sanding sugar (optional)
1 recipe Mascarpone Dream (optional)

1. Preheat oven to 375°F. For biscuits, in a medium bowl stir together flour, the ¼ cup granulated sugar, the baking powder, and salt. Using a pastry blender, cut in butter until pieces are pea size. Make a well in the center of biscuit mixture. Cover and chill while preparing filling.

2. For filling, in a Dutch oven combine cherries, the 2 cups granulated sugar, and the cornstarch. Cook over medium heat until cherries release their juices, stirring occasionally. Increase heat to medium-high; cook and stir until thickened and bubbly. Keep filling hot.

3. In a small bowl combine eggs, milk, almond extract, and vanilla. Add egg mixture, white chocolate, and almonds all at once to biscuit mixture. Using a fork, stir just until moistened.

4. Transfer hot filling to a 3-quart rectangular baking dish. Immediately drop biscuit dough into 12 to 16 mounds onto filling. If desired, sprinkle mounds with pearl sugar.

5. Bake for 25 to 30 minutes or until biscuits are golden. Cool on a wire rack about 1 hour. Serve warm. If desired, serve with Mascarpone Dream.

PER SERVING *540 cal., 20 g fat (10 g sat. fat), 60 mg chol., 272 mg sodium, 86 g carb., 4 g fiber, 8 g pro.*

Mascarpone Dream In a large mixing bowl beat 8 ounces softened mascarpone with a mixer on low for 30 seconds. Beat in 1 cup sugar. Gradually beat in 1 cup whipping cream and 1½ teaspoons almond extract until soft peaks form (tips curl). Use immediately or cover and chill up to 6 hours.

CHERRY COBBLER WITH WHITE CHOCOLATE-ALMOND BISCUITS

Pumpkin Bread Pudding Soufflé

PREP 45 minutes
BAKE 30 minutes at 375°F
MAKES 6 servings

- 1 to 2 tablespoons butter, softened
- 1 to 2 tablespoons granulated sugar
- 10 ounces challah
- 2 cups half-and-half or light cream
- ½ cup butter, softened
- ¼ cup packed brown sugar
- ½ teaspoon ground cinnamon
- ¼ teaspoon ground ginger
- ⅛ teaspoon freshly grated nutmeg
- 4 egg yolks
- 1 cup canned pumpkin
- 3 egg whites
- ¼ teaspoon cream of tartar
- 1 tablespoon sugar
- 1 recipe Easy Bourbon Molasses Sauce

1. Preheat oven to 375°F. Lightly coat six 10-ounce ramekins or custard cups with the 1 to 2 tablespoons softened butter; sprinkle lightly with the 1 to 2 tablespoons granulated sugar. Place ramekins in a 15×10×1-inch baking pan; set aside. Remove and discard the bottom and side crusts from challah. Cut challah into small cubes (about 4½ cups). Place cubes in a large bowl; set aside.

PUMPKIN BREAD
PUDDING SOUFFLÉ

2. In a small saucepan bring half-and-half to simmering over low heat. Pour 1 cup of the warm half-and-half over the challah cubes; stir gently. Set aside.
3. In a large mixing bowl beat the ½ cup butter with a mixer on medium to high for 30 seconds. Add brown sugar. Beat until light and fluffy, scraping sides of bowl occasionally. Beat in cinnamon, ginger, nutmeg, and egg yolks until combined. Beat in pumpkin and the remaining half-and-half. Add soaked challah cubes to the pumpkin mixture; fold in gently.
4. Wash beaters thoroughly. In another large mixing bowl beat egg whites and cream of tartar with a mixer on medium until soft peaks form (tips curl). Add the 1 tablespoon granulated sugar and beat until stiff peaks form (tips stand straight). Gently fold beaten egg whites into the challah mixture. Spoon mixture evenly into prepared ramekins.
5. Bake for 30 minutes or until a knife inserted into centers comes out clean. Serve warm with Easy Bourbon Molasses Sauce. Soufflés will fall slightly as they cool.

Easy Bourbon Molasses Sauce In a small saucepan combine 1½ cups sugar, ½ cup butter, ½ cup water, 2 tablespoons molasses, 2 egg yolks lightly beaten, and ¼ teaspoon salt. Whisk over medium heat just until sauce is thick and comes to a boil. Strain sauce into a 4-cup glass measure. Stir in ¼ cup bourbon (sauce will foam). Serve warm. Cover and chill any remaining sauce. To reheat, place in a microwave-safe bowl and heat on medium for 1 to 1½ minutes, stirring every 30 seconds.
PER SERVING 892 cal., 49 g fat (29 g sat. fat), 350 mg chol., 637 mg sodium, 99 g carb., 2 g fiber, 12 g pro.

Very Cherry Slab Pie

(photo page 74)

PREP 40 minutes
BAKE 45 minutes at 375°F
STAND 30 minutes
MAKES 24 servings

- 4 cups fresh or frozen pitted tart red cherries
- 3 cups fresh or frozen pitted dark sweet cherries
- 1½ cups sugar
- ⅓ cup all-purpose flour
- 1 cup dried cherries, halved
- 4 cups all-purpose flour
- 1 teaspoon salt
- ¾ cup shortening
- ¾ cup butter
- 2 egg yolks
  Cold water
- 1 egg, lightly beaten
- 1 tablespoon water

1. If using frozen cherries, let stand at room temperature for 30 minutes; drain. In an extra-large bowl stir together sugar and ⅓ cup flour. Add fresh or frozen cherries and dried cherries; toss gently to coat.
2. Preheat oven to 375°F. For pastry, in another extra-large bowl stir together 4 cups flour and salt. Using a pastry blender, cut in shortening and butter until mixture resembles coarse crumbs. In a glass measuring cup beat egg yolks with a fork. Stir in enough cold water to measure 1 cup total liquid. Add egg yolk mixture all at once to flour mixture. Stir lightly with fork until combined. Evenly divide pastry into three portions; combine two portions into one.
3. On a lightly floured surface, roll the large pastry portion into a 19×13-inch rectangle; trim edges to make an 18×12-inch rectangle. Wrap pastry rectangle around the rolling pin; unroll into a 15×10×1-inch baking pan (pastry will extend over edges of pan). Spoon cherry filling into pastry-lined baking pan.
4. Roll the remaining pastry portion into a 16×11-inch rectangle. Using a cookie cutter, cut shapes from pastry. Place pastry over filling. Bring edges of the bottom pastry up and over edges of top pastry; fold edges in slightly toward center. Seal edges with tines of fork. In a small bowl combine egg and 1 tablespoon water. Brush surface of pastry with egg mixture.
5. Bake for 45 to 50 minutes or until filling is bubbly and pastry is golden. Cool completely in pan on a wire rack.
PER SERVING 288 cal., 13 g fat (6 g sat. fat), 38 mg chol., 154 mg sodium, 41 g carb., 2 g fiber, 4 g pro.

SWEET POTATO MARSHMALLOW PIE

Sweet Potato Marshmallow Pie

PREP 30 minutes BAKE 14 minutes at 450°F / 35 minutes at 375°F
BROIL 1 minute MAKES 8 servings

- 1 recipe Pastry for Single-Crust Pie
- 2 cups mashed cooked sweet potatoes
- ¾ cup sugar
- 1 teaspoon pumpkin pie spice or ground cinnamon
- ¼ teaspoon salt
- 3 eggs, lightly beaten
- 1 cup buttermilk
- 1½ cups tiny marshmallows
- 1 cup pecans halves, toasted (see tip, page 19)
- 3 to 4 tablespoons caramel-flavor ice cream topping

1. Preheat oven to 450°F. Prepare Pastry for a Single-Crust Pie. On a lightly floured surface, use your hands to slightly flatten pastry. Roll pastry from center to edges into a circle about 12 inches in diameter. Wrap pastry around the rolling pin. Unroll into a 9-inch pie plate. Ease pastry into pie plate without stretching it. Trim pastry ½ inch beyond edge of pie plate. Fold under extra pastry even with the plate edge. Crimp edge as desired. Generously prick bottom and sides of pastry with a fork. Line pastry with a double thickness of foil. Bake for 8 minutes. Remove foil. Bake for 6 to 8 minutes more or until golden. Cool on a wire rack. Reduce oven temperature to 375°F.

2. For filling, in a large bowl combine mashed sweet potatoes, sugar, pumpkin pie spice, and salt. Add eggs; beat lightly with a fork just until combined. Gradually stir in buttermilk until combined.

3. Place pastry shell on the oven rack. Carefully pour filling into pastry shell. Bake for 35 to 40 minutes or until a knife inserted near center comes out clean. Cool completely on wire rack.

4. Before serving, preheat broiler. In a large bowl combine marshmallows and pecans; mound on top of pie. Broil 4 to 5 inches from the heat for 1 to 2 minutes or until marshmallows are softened and lightly browned. Drizzle with caramel topping.

Pastry for Single-Crust Pie In a medium bowl stir together 1½ cups flour and ½ teaspoon salt. Using a pastry blender, cut in ¼ cup shortening and ¼ cup butter, cut up, until pieces are pea size. Sprinkle 1 tablespoon ice water over part of the flour mixture; toss gently with a fork. Push moistened dough to side of bowl. Repeat with additional ice water, 1 tablespoon at a time (¼ to ⅓ cup total), until all of the flour mixture is moistened. Gather dough pastry into a ball, kneading gently until it holds together.

PER SERVING 501 cal., 23 g fat (7 g sat. fat), 86 mg chol., 385 mg sodium, 67 g carb., 4 g fiber, 9 g pro.

S'MORE
BROWNIE PIES

S'more Brownie Pies

PREP 45 minutes BAKE 22 minutes
at 350°F / 3 minutes at 450°F
CHILL 15 minutes MAKES 8 servings

¼ cup butter
1½ ounces unsweetened chocolate,
　coarsely chopped
　Nonstick cooking spray
1 cup finely crushed honey or
　cinnamon graham crackers
2 tablespoons sugar
¼ cup butter, melted
2 eggs, lightly beaten
¾ cup sugar
¼ cup all-purpose flour
½ teaspoon vanilla
⅛ teaspoon baking soda
¼ cup chopped pecans
¼ cup milk chocolate pieces
1 recipe Marshmallow Frosting

1. In a small heavy saucepan stir ¼ cup butter and unsweetened chocolate over low heat until melted. Cool for 20 minutes.
2. Meanwhile, preheat oven to 350°F. Lightly coat four 4×1-inch petite pie pans with cooking spray; set aside. For crusts, in a medium bowl stir together crushed graham crackers and 2 tablespoons sugar. Drizzle with ¼ cup melted butter; toss gently to combine. Divide mixture among the prepared pie pans, pressing evenly onto bottoms and up the sides; set aside.
3. For filling, in a medium bowl combine eggs, ¾ cup sugar, flour, vanilla, and baking soda. Stir in melted chocolate mixture, pecans, and milk chocolate pieces. Divide filling among crusts, spreading evenly. Bake for 22 to 25 minutes or until filling is evenly puffed and centers jiggle slightly when shaken, covering pies loosely with foil if necessary to prevent overbrowning. Cool on wire racks (centers may sink slightly).
4. Using a pastry bag fitted with a large star tip, pipe Marshmallow Frosting on pies, pulling up as you pipe to add high peaks to the frosting. Chill for 15 minutes.
5. Preheat oven to 450°F. Bake pies for 3 to 4 minutes or until frosting is lightly toasted. Cool on wire racks.
Marshmallow Frosting In the top of a 2-quart double boiler combine 1 cup sugar, ¼ cup cold water, 2 egg whites,

and ¼ teaspoon cream of tartar. Beat with a mixer on low for 30 seconds. Place the double boiler top over boiling water (upper pan should not touch water). Cook, beating constantly with the mixer on high, for 10 to 13 minutes or until an instant-read thermometer registers 160°F. Remove pan from heat. Add 1 teaspoon vanilla. Beat for 1 minute or until frosting is fluffy and holds soft peaks (tips curl).
PER SERVING *463 cal., 22 g fat (11 g sat. fat), 80 mg chol., 221 mg sodium, 67 g carb., 2 g fiber, 5 g pro.*

Ginger Fig Tarts with Honey-Mascarpone Cream

PREP 30 minutes STAND 30 minutes
BAKE 15 minutes at 350°F
COOL 35 minutes
MAKES 12 servings

¾ cup sugar
¾ cup water
3 tablespoons finely chopped
　crystallized ginger
9 ounces dried Calimyrna figs,
　stemmed and coarsely chopped
8 sheets frozen phyllo dough
　(14×9-inch rectangles), thawed
¼ cup butter, melted
1 recipe Honey-Mascarpone Cream
　Honey (optional)

1. For filling, in a medium saucepan combine sugar, the water, and ginger. Bring to boiling over medium heat, stirring to dissolve sugar. Stir in figs. Boil gently, uncovered, for 12 minutes; remove from heat. Cover and let stand for 30 minutes.
2. Meanwhile, preheat oven to 350°F. Grease twelve 2½-inch muffin cups; set aside. Unfold phyllo dough; cover with plastic wrap. (As you work, keep the phyllo covered to prevent it from drying out; remove sheets as you need them.) Place one sheet of phyllo on a work surface; brush lightly with some of the melted butter. Top with a second sheet of phyllo. Repeat brushing and layering two more times (four sheets total). Brush top lightly with melted butter.
3. Cut phyllo stack in half lengthwise. Cut each half crosswise into three squares, making six squares. Repeat with the remaining phyllo sheets and

butter to make 12 squares total. Gently press squares into prepared muffin cups, pleating to fit.
4. Bake for 10 minutes. Spoon filling evenly into phyllo cups. Bake for 5 to 10 minutes or until phyllo is golden. Cool in muffin cups on a wire rack for 5 minutes. Remove from muffin cups; cool completely on wire rack. Before serving, top tarts with Honey-Mascarpone Cream. If desired, drizzle with honey.
PER SERVING *261 cal., 11 g fat (7 g sat. fat), 32 mg chol., 98 mg sodium, 39 g carb., 3 g fiber, 3 g pro.*

Honey-Mascarpone Cream In a medium bowl stir together ⅓ cup softened mascarpone and 1 tablespoon honey until smooth. In another medium bowl whisk ½ cup whipping cream until soft peaks form (tips curl). Add one-third of the whipped cream to the mascarpone mixture. Stir until combined to lighten. Fold in the remaining whipped cream.

GINGER FIG TARTS WITH HONEY-MASCARPONE CREAM

EGGNOG AND RUM FUDGE PIE

Eggnog and Rum Fudge Pie

PREP 1 hour FREEZE 16 hours
COOL 30 minutes
BAKE 3 minutes at 475°F
MAKES 12 servings

- 1 recipe Chocolate Crumb Crust
- 1 cup sugar
- 1 5-ounce can evaporated milk
- 2 tablespoons butter
- 2 ounces unsweetened chocolate, chopped
- 1 teaspoon vanilla
- 2 pints eggnog ice cream
- 2 tablespoons dark rum (optional)
- ¾ cup sugar
- ½ cup boiling water
- ¼ cup meringue powder
- ⅓ cup toffee bits, crushed

1. Prepare Chocolate Crumb Crust. For fudge sauce, in a small saucepan combine the 1 cup granulated sugar, the evaporated milk, butter, and chocolate. Cook and stir over medium heat until bubbly; reduce heat. Boil gently for 4 to 5 minutes or until sauce is thickened and reduced to 1½ cups, stirring occasionally. Remove from heat; stir in vanilla. Transfer to a medium bowl; beat with a mixer on medium until almost smooth. Cover with plastic wrap. Cool completely.
2. In a chilled bowl stir 1 pint of the ice cream until softened. If desired, stir in

1 tablespoon of the rum. Spread over cooled Chocolate Crumb Crust. Spoon half the fudge sauce in small spoonfuls over ice cream. Freeze for 2 hours or until nearly firm. Repeat with the remaining ice cream, rum (if desired), and fudge sauce. Return to freezer.
3. For meringue, in a bowl stir together the ¾ cup sugar and the boiling water until sugar is dissolved. Cool to room temperature (about 30 minutes). Add the meringue powder. Beat with a mixer on low until combined; beat on high until stiff peaks form (tips stand straight). Fold 3 tablespoons of the crushed toffee bits into the meringue. Spread meringue over pie, sealing to edge. Freeze for 6 hours or until firm.
4. Preheat oven to 475°F. Bake for 3 to 4 minutes or just until meringue is light brown. Cover loosely with foil. Freeze for 6 to 24 hours before serving. Before serving, sprinkle with the remaining crushed toffee bits.
Chocolate Crumb Crust Preheat oven to 375°F. Lightly coat an 8-inch springform pan with nonstick cooking spray. In a bowl combine 1 cup finely crushed vanilla wafers, ⅓ cup powdered sugar, and 3 tablespoons unsweetened cocoa powder. Stir in 3 tablespoons melted butter. Press into the bottom of pan. Bake for 7 minutes or until crust is firm. Cool in pan on a wire rack.
PER SERVING *546 cal., 24 g fat (14 g sat. fat), 83 mg chol., 161 mg sodium, 82 g carb., 2 g fiber, 5 g pro.*

Creamy Cranberry Pretzel Pie

PREP 30 minutes
BAKE 7 minutes at 350°F
CHILL 4 hours MAKES 8 servings

   Nonstick cooking spray
- ½ cup butter
- ½ cup sugar
- 1¼ cups finely crushed pretzel sticks (about 4 ounces)
- 1 egg white
- 1½ cups whipping cream
- 12 ounces cream cheese, softened
- 1 14-ounce can whole berry cranberry sauce
- 1 tablespoon finely shredded orange peel
   Few drops red food coloring
   Broken pretzel sticks (optional)
   Sugared cranberries* (optional)

1. Preheat oven to 350°F. Lightly coat a 9-inch pie plate with cooking spray; set aside. For crust, in a medium saucepan melt butter over medium heat. Remove from heat. Stir in ¼ cup of the sugar until dissolved. Add crushed pretzels, stirring to combine. Stir in egg white until combined. Press crust evenly onto the bottom and up the sides of the prepared pie plate. Bake for 7 to 9 minutes or until edges are lightly browned. Cool on a wire rack.
2. Meanwhile, for filling, in a medium mixing bowl beat whipping cream with a mixer on medium to high until stiff peaks form (tips stand straight); set aside. In a large mixing bowl beat cream cheese and the remaining ¼ cup sugar on medium until smooth. In a small bowl stir together cranberry sauce and orange peel until no large clumps remain; stir into cream cheese mixture until combined. Fold in whipped cream and food coloring. Carefully spoon filling into baked crust.
3. Cover and chill pie for 4 to 6 hours or until firm. If desired, garnish with broken pretzels and sugared cranberries.
PER SERVING *579 cal., 43 g fat (26 g sat. fat), 139 mg chol., 566 mg sodium, 47 g carb., 1 g fiber, 5 g pro.*
*Tip To make sugared cranberries, coat ⅓ cup fresh cranberries with light-color corn syrup, then roll in sugar.

CREAMY
CRANBERRY
PRETZEL PIE

The Cookie Collection

SAY CHRISTMAS sweetly with batches of
homemade cookies. Fill trays, jars, and gift boxes
with treats of every shape and flavor—simple or

SUGAR COOKIE
CUTOUTS, PAGE 101.

93

Dark Chocolate Stars

PREP **30 minutes** CHILL **1 hour**
BAKE **7 minutes at 375°F**
MAKES **about 36 large and 18 small sandwich cookies**

- 1 cup butter, softened
- 1½ cups unsweetened cocoa powder
- 1¼ cups sugar
- 4 ounces dark chocolate, melted and cooled
- ½ teaspoon baking powder
- ½ teaspoon salt
- 2 eggs
- 1 tablespoon milk
- 1½ teaspoons vanilla
- 1½ cups all-purpose flour
- 1 recipe Fudge Filling or 1 cup hot fudge- or chocolate-flavor ice cream topping
- 3 ounces dark chocolate, melted (optional)
  Unsweetened cocoa powder (optional)

1. In a large mixing bowl beat butter with a mixer on medium to high for 30 seconds. Add the 1½ cups cocoa powder, the sugar, the 4 ounces melted chocolate, baking powder, and salt. Beat until combined, scraping sides of bowl occasionally. Beat in eggs, milk, and vanilla until combined. Beat in as much of the flour as you can with the mixer. Using a wooden spoon, stir in any remaining flour. Divide dough in half. Cover and chill about 1 hour or until dough is easy to handle.
2. Preheat oven to 375°F. On a lightly floured surface,* roll half of the dough at a time to ⅛-inch thickness. Using a 2½- to 3-inch star-shape cookie cutter, cut out dough. Using a 1-inch star-shape cookie cutter, cut and remove a star from the center of half the cookies.
3. Place cutouts 2 inches apart on an ungreased cookie sheet. Bake for 7 to 8 minutes or until edges are firm. Transfer to a wire rack; cool.
4. Spread Fudge Filling on bottoms of the large cookies without cutout centers. Top with the large cookies with cutout centers, bottom sides down. Spread Fudge Filling on bottoms of half the small cookies. Top with the remaining small cookies,

DARK CHOCOLATE STARS

bottom sides down. If desired, drizzle or spread cookies with 3 ounces melted chocolate and sprinkle with cocoa powder.

Fudge Filling In a small saucepan stir ½ cup dark chocolate or semisweet chocolate pieces over low heat until melted. Cool slightly. In a small bowl combine 3 ounces cream cheese and ⅓ cup powdered sugar. Stir in melted chocolate and ¼ teaspoon vanilla. If necessary, stir in enough hot water, 1 teaspoon at a time, until filling reaches spreading consistency.

PER SERVING *128 cal., 8 g fat (5 g sat. fat), 23 mg chol., 85 mg sodium, 16 g carb., 2 g fiber, 2 g pro.*

*Tip If desired, roll dough on a surface lightly coated with a mix of flour and unsweetened cocoa powder.

Peppermint Palmiers

PREP **45 minutes**
CHILL **5 hours** FREEZE **4 hours**
BAKE **10 minutes at 350°F**
MAKES **80 servings**

½ cup butter, softened
½ cup granulated sugar
½ cup packed brown sugar
½ teaspoon baking powder
¼ teaspoon salt
1 egg
2 tablespoons white crème de menthe
1 tablespoon milk
½ teaspoon vanilla
2¾ cups all-purpose flour
1 8-ounce package cream cheese, softened
½ cup powdered sugar
¼ cup all-purpose flour
1 tablespoon white crème de menthe
Few drops red food coloring
½ cup finely crushed peppermint candies

1. In a large mixing bowl beat butter with a mixer on medium to high for 30 seconds. Add granulated sugar, brown sugar, baking powder, and salt. Beat until combined, scraping sides of bowl occasionally. Beat in egg, the 2 tablespoons crème de menthe, milk, and vanilla. Beat in as much of the 2¾ cups flour as you can with the

PEPPERMINT PALMIERS

mixer. Using a wooden spoon, stir in any of the remaining 2¾ cups flour. Divide dough in half. Cover and chill about 3 hours or until dough is easy to handle.
2. Meanwhile, for filling, in a medium mixing bowl beat cream cheese, powdered sugar, the ¼ cup flour, and the 1 tablespoon crème de menthe on low to medium until smooth. Stir in enough red food coloring to tint pale pink. Gently fold in crushed candies. Cover and chill for up to 2 hours. (Do not chill longer than 2 hours or the candies will bleed into the filling and the filling will become too soft and sticky.)
3. On a lightly floured surface, roll one portion at a time into a 12×8-inch rectangle. Spread half of the filling over rolled dough to within ½ inch

of each long edge. Roll up both long edges, scroll fashion, to meet in the center. Brush seam where dough spirals meet with water; lightly press together. Wrap each scroll in plastic wrap; place on a tray or cookie sheet. Freeze 4 to 24 hours or until firm.
4. Preheat oven to 350°F. Line a cookie sheet with parchment paper; set aside. Using a serrated knife, cut scrolls into ¼-inch slices. Place slices 2 inches apart on the prepared cookie sheet. Bake for 10 minutes or until edges are firm and bottoms are light brown. Transfer cookies to a wire rack; cool.
PER SERVING *53 cal., 2 g fat (1 g sat. fat), 9 mg chol., 27 mg sodium, 8 g carb., 0 g fiber, 1 g pro.*

Crunchy Milk Chocolate-Almond Roll

PREP 26 minutes   CHILL 3 hours
STAND 5 minutes
BAKE 6 minutes at 350°F
MAKES 28 servings

- ½ cup slivered almonds
- 8 vanilla wafers, coarsely chopped (about ½ cup)
- 1 11.5-ounce package milk chocolate pieces
- 6 tablespoons butter
- ¼ cup cold, strong brewed coffee
- ¼ teaspoon salt
- ⅓ cup finely snipped dried apricots
- ½ teaspoon finely shredded orange peel
- ¼ cup powdered sugar
- ¼ cup unsweetened cocoa powder

1. Preheat oven to 350°F. Spread almonds and chopped wafers in a single layer in a shallow baking pan. Bake about 6 minutes or until nuts and wafers are lightly toasted; cool.

2. In a small heavy saucepan stir chocolate pieces and butter over low heat until melted and smooth. In a medium bowl combine coffee and salt, stirring to dissolve salt. Stir coffee mixture into chocolate mixture. Fold in almonds and wafers, dried apricots, and orange peel. Transfer to the medium bowl. Cover and chill for 1 to 1½ hours or until dough is firm but malleable.

3. Divide dough in half. On a sheet of waxed paper, shape half the dough at a time into a 7×2-inch log. Wrap log in waxed paper, twisting ends to seal. Gently roll log back and forth to make it perfectly round. Chill for 2 to 3 hours or until firm.

4. Unwrap logs; let stand for 5 minutes. In a shallow dish stir together powdered sugar and cocoa powder. Using a serrated knife, cut logs into ½-inch slices. Roll edges of slices in cocoa powder mixture. Serve at once or chill until ready to serve.

PER SERVING *105 cal., 7 g fat (4 g sat. fat), 10 mg chol., 56 mg sodium, 10 g carb., 1 g fiber, 1 g pro.*

Dark Chocolate and Espresso Cookie Coins with Smoked Salt

PREP 30 minutes   CHILL 3 hours
BAKE 10 minutes at 325°F
MAKES 60 cookies

- 1 tablespoon hot water
- 1 tablespoon instant espresso coffee powder
- 1 cup butter, softened
- ¾ cup powdered sugar
- 1 teaspoon vanilla
- ¼ teaspoon salt
- 1¾ cups all-purpose flour
- 4 ounces bittersweet chocolate, finely chopped
- 4 ounces bittersweet chocolate, chopped
- 1 tablespoon shortening
  Coarse smoked sea salt flakes or sea salt, slightly crushed

1. In a small bowl stir the hot water into coffee powder until dissolved; set aside. In a large mixing bowl beat butter and powdered sugar with a mixer on medium for 30 seconds. Beat on medium-high for 3 minutes more. Beat in coffee mixture, vanilla, and the ¼ teaspoon salt until combined. Gradually add flour, beating on low just until combined. Using a wooden spoon, stir in the 4 ounces finely chopped chocolate.

2. Divide dough in half. Shape each portion into a 10-inch log. Wrap each log in plastic wrap or waxed paper. Chill for 3 hours or until dough is firm enough to slice.

3. Preheat oven to 325°F. Line a cookie sheet with parchment paper. Using a serrated knife, cut rolls into ¼-inch slices. Place slices 2 inches apart on the prepared cookie sheet. Bake for 10 to 12 minutes or until cookies are set. Transfer to a wire rack; cool.

4. In a small saucepan stir the 4 ounces chopped chocolate and shortening over low heat until melted and smooth. Dip half of each cookie into melted chocolate, allowing excess to drip back into pan. Return cookies to wire rack. Sprinkle lightly with sea salt. Let stand until chocolate is set.

PER 2 COOKIES *135 cal., 10 g fat (6 g sat. fat), 16 mg chol., 152 mg sodium, 13 g carb., 1 g fiber, 1 g pro.*

CRUNCHY MILK CHOCOLATE-ALMOND ROLL

DARK CHOCOLATE AND
ESPRESSO COOKIE
COINS WITH SMOKED
SALT

APRICOT PINWHEELS

Apricot Pinwheels

PREP 35 minutes   CHILL overnight
BAKE 9 minutes at 400°F
MAKES 27 servings

- 1 8-ounce package cream cheese, softened
- 1 cup butter, softened
- 2½ cups all-purpose flour
- ¼ teaspoon salt
- ⅔ cup apricot preserves
- 1 egg, lightly beaten
  Coarse sanding sugar

1. In a large mixing bowl beat cream cheese and butter with a mixer on medium to high about 3 minutes or until very light and fluffy, scraping sides of bowl occasionally. Gradually beat in flour and salt. Form dough into a ball and knead until smooth. Divide dough into thirds. Cover and chill overnight.

2. Preheat oven to 400°F. Line a cookie sheet with parchment paper; set aside. Remove dough, one portion at a time, from the refrigerator and place on a lightly floured surface. Roll dough into a 9-inch square. Cut rolled dough into nine 3-inch squares.

3. Place squares 1 inch apart on the prepared cookie sheet. Cut 1-inch slits from the corners toward the center of each square. Spoon about 1 teaspoon of the preserves into each center. Brush dough lightly with beaten egg. Fold every other tip (one from each corner) to the center to form a pinwheel, pressing tips gently to seal.

4. Brush lightly with the remaining beaten egg and sprinkle with sanding sugar. Bake for 9 to 10 minutes or just until golden and slightly puffed. Transfer cookies to a wire rack; cool.

PER SERVING *157 cal., 10 g fat (6 g sat. fat), 34 mg chol., 114 mg sodium, 15 g carb., 0 g fiber, 2 g pro.*

Brown Sugar-Hazelnut Spirals

PREP 40 minutes   CHILL 1 hour
BAKE 8 minutes at 375°F
MAKES 72 servings

- 1 cup butter, softened
- ¾ cup granulated sugar
- ¾ cup packed brown sugar
- 1½ teaspoons baking powder
- ½ teaspoon salt
- 1 egg
- 1 teaspoon vanilla
- 2½ cups all-purpose flour
- ⅓ cup chocolate-hazelnut spread
- ¼ cup ground hazelnuts (filberts)

1. In a large mixing bowl beat butter with a mixer on medium to high for 30 seconds. Add granulated sugar, brown sugar, baking powder, and salt. Beat until combined, scraping sides of bowl occasionally. Beat in egg and vanilla until combined. Beat in as much of the flour as you can with the mixer. Using a wooden spoon, stir in any remaining flour.

2. Divide dough in half. Leave one half plain. Stir chocolate-hazelnut spread and hazelnuts into the remaining half. Divide each portion in half again, making four portions total.

3. On a sheet of waxed paper, roll each portion of dough into an 8×7-inch rectangle. Using the waxed paper, invert one chocolate dough rectangle on top of one plain dough rectangle. Roll dough together into a 10×8-inch rectangle. Peel off top sheet of waxed paper. Starting from a long side, tightly roll up dough into a spiral log; seal edge. Wrap each log in plastic wrap. Chill for 1 to 2 hours or until dough is firm enough to slice.

4. Preheat oven to 375°F. Cut logs into ¼-inch slices. Place slices 2 inches apart on an ungreased cookie sheet. Bake for 8 to 10 minutes or until edges are firm and light brown. Cool on cookie sheet for 1 minute. Transfer cookies to a wire rack; cool.

PER SERVING *66 cal., 3 g fat (2 g sat. fat), 9 mg chol., 51 mg sodium, 9 g carb., 0 g fiber, 1 g pro.*

Candied Ginger and Orange Icebox Cookies

PREP **30 minutes**
CHILL **2 hours**
BAKE **8 minutes at 350°F**
MAKES **70 servings**

½ cup butter, softened
¾ cup granulated sugar
1½ teaspoons baking powder
⅛ teaspoon salt
1 egg
1 tablespoon milk
2 cups all-purpose flour
⅓ cup finely chopped crystallized ginger
2 teaspoons finely shredded orange peel
¼ cup coarse sugar
  Milk

1. In a large mixing bowl beat butter with a mixer on medium to high for 30 seconds. Add granulated sugar, baking powder, and salt. Beat until

combined, scraping sides of bowl occasionally. Beat in egg and the 1 tablespoon milk until combined. Beat in as much of the flour as you can with the mixer. Using a wooden spoon, stir in any remaining flour, the crystallized ginger, and orange peel. If necessary, use your hands to knead dough until it comes together.

2. Divide dough into three portions. On a lightly floured surface, shape each portion into a 7-inch logs. Spread coarse sugar on waxed paper. Roll each log in coarse sugar to coat, pressing lightly as you log (you won't use all of the sugar). If necessary, reshape rolls.

Wrap each in waxed paper or plastic wrap. Chill for 2 to 3 hours or until dough is firm enough to slice.

3. Preheat oven to 350°F. Cut logs into ¼-inch slices. Place slices 1 inch apart on an ungreased cookie sheet. Brush lightly with additional milk and sprinkle with the remaining coarse sugar.

4. Bake for 8 minutes or until edges are light brown. Transfer cookies to a wire rack; cool.

PER SERVING *43 cal., 2 g fat (1 g sat. fat), 7 mg chol., 29 mg sodium, 7 g carb., 0 g fiber, 1 g pro.*

CANDIED GINGER AND ORANGE ICEBOX COOKIES

PEPPERED-ORANGE
GINGERBREAD
CUTOUTS

Peppered-Orange Gingerbread Cutouts

PREP 30 minutes CHILL 4 hours
BAKE 6 minutes at 375°F
STAND 1 hour MAKES 25 servings

½ cup shortening
½ cup sugar
1 teaspoon baking powder
1 teaspoon ground ginger
½ teaspoon baking soda
½ teaspoon ground cinnamon
½ teaspoon ground cloves
¼ teaspoon cayenne pepper
½ cup molasses
1 egg
1 tablespoon vinegar
1½ teaspoons finely shredded orange peel
2½ cups all-purpose flour
   Nonstick cooking spray
1 recipe Royal Icing (see recipe, right)

1. In a mixing bowl beat shortening with a mixer on medium to high for 30 seconds. Add sugar, baking powder, ginger, baking soda, cinnamon, cloves, and cayenne pepper. Beat until combined, scraping bowl. Beat in the molasses, egg, vinegar, and orange peel until combined. Beat in as much of the flour as you can with the mixer. Stir in remaining flour. Divide dough in half. Cover and chill for at least 4 hours or until easy to handle.
2. Preheat oven to 375°F. Line cookie sheets with parchment paper; set aside. On a lightly floured surface, roll half the dough at a time to ⅛-inches thick. Cut shapes using 3- to 4-inch gingerbread people cookie cutters. Place cutouts 1 inch apart on prepared cookie sheets. Chill and reroll scraps as necessary. Keep dough chilled because it softens quickly.
3. Bake for 6 minutes or until edges are lightly browned. Cool on cookie sheet 1 minute. Transfer cookies to a wire rack to cool.
4. Decorate with Royal Icing (recipe at right).

PER SERVING 263 cal., 7 g fat (2 g sat. fat), 13 mg chol., 77 mg sodium, 47 g carb., 1 g fiber, 3 g pro.

SUGAR COOKIE CUTOUTS

Sugar Cookie Cutouts

PREP 40 minutes CHILL 1 hour
BAKE 7 minutes at 375°F
MAKES 36 servings

⅔ cup butter, softened
¾ cup granulated sugar
1 teaspoon baking powder
¼ teaspoon salt
1 egg
1 tablespoon milk
1 teaspoon vanilla
2 cups all-purpose flour
1 recipe Powdered Sugar Icing (optional)
1 recipe Royal Icing (optional)

1. In a large mixing bowl beat butter with a mixer on medium to high for 30 seconds. Add granulated sugar, baking powder, and salt. Beat until combined, scraping sides of bowl occasionally. Beat in egg, milk, and vanilla until combined. Beat in as much of the flour as you can with the mixer. Stir in any remaining flour. Divide dough in half. Cover and chill for 1 to 2 hours or until dough is easy to handle.
2. Preheat oven to 375°F. On a lightly floured surface, roll half the dough at a time to ⅛- to ¼-inch thickness.

Using 2½-inch cookie cutters, cut out shapes. Place cutouts 1 inch apart on ungreased cookie sheets.
3. Bake for 7 to 10 minutes or until edges are firm and bottoms are very light brown. Transfer cookies to a wire rack to cool. Decorate with Powdered Sugar and/or Royal Icing. Let stand until set.

PER SERVING 74 cal., 4 g fat (2 g sat. fat), 15 mg chol., 59 mg sodium, 10 g carb., 0 g fiber, 1 g pro.

Powdered Sugar Icing In a small bowl combine 3 cups powdered sugar, ½ teaspoon vanilla or almond extract, and enough milk (6 to 8 teaspoons) to make a smooth drizzling consistency. Makes about 1 cup.

Royal Icing In a large mixing bowl stir together one 16-ounce package powdered sugar, 3 tablespoons meringue powder, and ½ teaspoon cream of tartar. Add ½ cup warm water and 1 teaspoon vanilla. Beat with a mixer on low until combined; beat on high for 7 to 10 minutes or until icing reaches a stiff piping consistency. If not using right away, cover bowl with a damp paper towel and cover paper towel with plastic wrap; chill up to 48 hours.

Lemon Ladyfinger Sandwich Cookies

PREP 45 minutes
BAKE 5 minutes at 425°F
COOL 10 minutes
MAKES 20 servings

  6 egg whites
 ⅔ cup granulated sugar
  5 egg yolks
  2 tablespoons granulated sugar
  1 teaspoon vanilla
  1 cup all-purpose flour
  2 teaspoons finely shredded lemon peel
  2 tablespoons powdered sugar
  1 8-ounce package cream cheese, softened
 ½ cup lemon curd
  5 cups powdered sugar

1. Preheat oven to 425°F. Line three large cookie sheets with parchment paper; set aside. In a large mixing bowl beat egg whites with a mixer on medium until soft peaks form (tips curl). Gradually add the ⅔ cup granulated sugar, about 1 tablespoon at a time, beating on high until stiff peaks form (tips stand straight). Set aside.
2. In a medium mixing bowl beat egg yolks and the 2 tablespoons granulated sugar on high about 5 minutes or until mixture is thick. Beat in vanilla.
3. Fold egg yolk mixture into beaten egg whites just until combined.

Sprinkle ⅓ cup of the flour over egg mixture; fold in gently just until combined. Repeat with the remaining flour, ⅓ cup at a time, being careful not to overmix. Fold in lemon peel.
4. Spoon about one-third of the batter into a decorating bag fitted with a ½-inch round tip.* Pipe batter into 3×1-inch logs, 1 inch apart, onto one of the prepared cookie sheets. Sprinkle logs lightly with some of the 2 tablespoons powdered sugar. (Wait to pipe the remaining batter until just before baking so the batter does not deflate while standing.)
5. Bake for 5 to 6 minutes or until light brown. Cool on cookie sheet for 10 minutes. Transfer cookies to a wire rack; cool.
6. For filling, in a medium mixing bowl beat cream cheese with a mixer on medium to high for 30 seconds. Beat in lemon curd until combined. Beat in enough of the 5 cups powdered sugar to reach piping consistency.
7. Spoon filling into a decorating bag fitted with a small round tip. Pipe filling onto bottoms of half the cookies. Top with the remaining cookies, bottom sides down.

PER SERVING *258 cal., 5 g fat (3 g sat. fat), 65 mg chol., 62 mg sodium, 50 g carb., 1 g fiber, 3 g pro.*
*Tip If you don't have a ½-inch round tip, spoon batter into a heavy resealable plastic bag then snip off ½ inch from one corner of the bag.

LEMON LADYFINGER SANDWICH COOKIES

Shortbread Pizza Cookie

PREP 20 minutes
BAKE 25 minutes at 325°F
MAKES 12 servings

 2½ cups all-purpose flour
 ⅓ cup granulated sugar
  1 cup butter
  2 teaspoons finely shredded orange peel or lemon peel (optional)

1. Preheat oven to 325°F. In a large bowl stir together flour and sugar. Using a pastry blender, cut in butter until mixture resembles fine crumbs and starts to cling. If desired, stir in orange peel. Using your hands, form dough into a ball and knead until smooth. Slightly flatten ball.

2. Place dough on an ungreased cookie sheet and cover with waxed paper. Roll dough into a 10-inch circle; remove waxed paper. Crimp dough to make a scalloped edge. Cut circle into 12 wedges; leaving wedges intact.

3. Bake for 25 to 30 minutes or until bottom just starts to brown and center is set. Recut wedges while warm. Cool on cookie sheet for 5 minutes. Transfer to a wire rack; cool.

PER SERVING *252 cal., 16 g fat (10 g sat. fat), 41 mg chol., 136 mg sodium, 25 g carb., 1 g fiber, 3 g pro.*

Salted Nut Shortbread Pizza Cookie Prepare and cool Shortbread Pizza Cookie as directed. In a small saucepan stir 24 unwrapped vanilla caramels and 2 tablespoons whipping cream over low heat until smooth. Spread shortbread wedges with two-thirds of the caramel mixture. Top with two-thirds of a 7-ounce jar marshmallow creme, spreading evenly. Sprinkle with ¼ cup cocktail peanuts or salted cashews and drizzle with the remaining caramel mixture.

Pistachio-Fruit Shortbread Pizza Cookie Prepare and cool Shortbread Pizza Cookie as directed. Spread wedges with 3 ounces melted white baking chocolate with cocoa butter. Top with ¼ cup chopped pistachio nuts, 2 tablespoons snipped dried cranberries or tart cherries, and 2 tablespoons snipped dried apricots. Drizzle with 1 ounce additional melted white baking chocolate with cocoa butter.

Black Forest Shortbread Pizza Cookie Prepare and cool Shortbread Pizza Cookie as directed. Spread wedges with ¾ cup chocolate frosting. Sprinkle with ¾ cup chopped maraschino cherries (drained and patted dry) and ¼ cup sliced almonds. Top with spoonfuls of whipped cream and sprinkle with chocolate jimmies.

PISTACHIO-FRUIT SHORTBREAD PIZZA COOKIE

BLACK FOREST SHORTBREAD PIZZA COOKIE

SALTED NUT SHORTBREAD PIZZA COOKIE

**MINI RASPBERRY AND
WHITE CHOCOLATE
WHOOPIE PIES**

Mini Raspberry and White Chocolate Whoopie Pies

PREP 1 hour BAKE 7 minutes at 375°F
CHILL 30 minutes
MAKES 72 servings

½ cup butter, softened
1 cup granulated sugar
½ teaspoon baking soda
¼ teaspoon salt
1 egg
1 teaspoon vanilla
2 cups all-purpose flour
½ cup buttermilk or sour milk*
1 recipe White Chocolate and Mascarpone Filling
½ cup seedless raspberry preserves

1. Preheat oven to 375°F. Line a baking sheet with parchment paper; set aside.
2. In a large mixing bowl beat butter with a mixer on medium to high for 30 seconds. Add sugar, baking soda, and salt. Beat until combined, scraping sides of bowl occasionally. Beat in egg and vanilla until combined. Alternately add flour and buttermilk to butter mixture, beating on low after each addition just until combined. Drop dough by rounded teaspoons 1 inch apart onto the prepared cookie sheet.
3. Bake for 7 to 8 minutes or until tops are set. Cool on baking sheet on a wire rack.
4. Spoon White Chocolate and Mascarpone Filling into a large decorating bag fitted with a small star tip. Peel cooled cookies off parchment paper. Spread about ¼ teaspoon of the raspberry preserves onto bottoms of half the cookies; pipe filling onto preserves. Top with the remaining cookies, bottom sides down. Chill for 30 minutes before serving.
White Chocolate and Mascarpone Filling In a heavy small saucepan combine 3 ounces chopped white baking chocolate with cocoa butter and ¼ cup whipping cream. Stir over low heat until chocolate is nearly melted. Remove from heat; stir until smooth. Cool for 15 minutes. Meanwhile, in a large bowl combine ½ cup mascarpone or cream cheese and ¼ cup softened butter. Beat with a mixer on medium to high until smooth. Beat in ½ teaspoon

MALTED MILK CHOCOLATE TASSIES

vanilla. Gradually add 4 cups powdered sugar, beating well. Beat in the cooled white chocolate mixture. Chill for 30 minutes or until firm enough to pipe.
PER SERVING *91 cal., 3 g fat (2 g sat. fat), 11 mg chol., 39 mg sodium, 15 g carb., 0 g fiber, 1 g pro.*
* To make ½ cup sour milk place ½ cup 2% milk in a glass measure. Add 1½ teaspoons cider vinegar or lemon juice. Let stand for 5 minutes.

Malted Milk Chocolate Tassies

PREP 30 minutes CHILL 30 minutes
BAKE 8 minutes at 375°F
COOL 5 minutes MAKES 24 servings

1 cup all-purpose flour
¼ cup sugar
¼ cup malted milk powder
¼ cup unsweetened cocoa powder
½ cup butter
1 egg yolk, lightly beaten
2 tablespoons cold water
1 recipe Cream Filling
   Chopped malted milk balls

1. In a medium bowl stir together flour, sugar, malted milk powder, and cocoa powder. Using a pastry blender, cut in butter until mixture is crumbly. In a small bowl combine egg yolk and the cold water. Gradually stir egg yolk mixture into flour mixture. Gently knead dough just until a ball forms.

Cover and chill for 30 to 60 minutes or until dough is easy to handle.
2. Preheat oven to 375°F. Shape dough into 24 balls. Press balls onto the bottoms and up the sides of 24 ungreased 1¾-inch muffin cups. Bake for 8 to 10 minutes or until pastry is firm. If the centers puff during baking, press with the back of a measuring teaspoon while tassies are still warm. Cool in muffin cups on a wire rack for 5 minutes. Remove tassies from muffin cups. Cool completely on wire rack.
3. Spoon Cream Filling into a decorating bag fitted with an open star tip. Pipe filling into tassies (you will have more filling than you need). Sprinkle with chopped malted milk balls.
Cream Filling In a medium mixing bowl beat ¼ cup softened butter with a mixer on medium to high for 30 seconds. Add a 7-ounce jar marshmallow creme and 1 teaspoon vanilla; beat on medium until smooth. Beat in 1½ cups powdered sugar and 1 tablespoon milk. Gradually beat in 2 cups powdered sugar and enough additional milk to reach piping consistency.
PER SERVING *197 cal., 7 g fat (4 g sat. fat), 24 mg chol., 76 mg sodium, 34 g carb., 0 g fiber, 1 g pro.*

SALTED-PEANUT BLOSSOMS

Salted-Peanut Blossoms

PREP 25 minutes
BAKE 10 minutes at 350°F
MAKES 42 servings

½ cup shortening
½ cup peanut butter
¾ cup granulated sugar
½ cup packed brown sugar
1 teaspoon baking powder
⅛ teaspoon baking soda
1 egg
2 tablespoons milk
1 teaspoon vanilla
1¾ cups all-purpose flour
2 2.2-ounce salted peanut-coated caramel-topped nougat bars, such as Salted Nut Rolls, each cut into 24 slices

1. Preheat oven to 350°F. In a large mixing bowl beat shortening and peanut butter with a mixer on medium to high for 30 seconds. Add ½ cup of the granulated sugar, the brown sugar, baking powder, and baking soda. Beat until combined, scraping sides of bowl occasionally. Beat in egg, milk, and vanilla until combined. Beat in as much of the flour as you can with the mixer. Using a wooden spoon, stir in any remaining flour.
2. Shape dough into 1-inch balls. Roll balls in the remaining ¼ cup granulated sugar to coat. Place balls 2 inches apart on an ungreased cookie sheet. Bake for 10 to 12 minutes or until edges are firm and bottoms are light brown.
3. Immediately press a slice of peanut-coated nougat bar into each cookie center. Transfer cookies to a wire rack to cool.

PER SERVING *87 cal., 4 g fat (1 g sat. fat), 4 mg chol., 36 mg sodium, 11 g carb., 0 g fiber, 2 g pro.*

White Chocolate, Cornmeal, and Almond Mini Biscotti

PREP 35 minutes BAKE 20 minutes at 375°F / 16 minutes at 325°F
COOL 2 hours MAKES 42 servings

¾ cup butter, softened
½ cup granulated sugar
1 teaspoon baking powder
1 egg
1 teaspoon vanilla
1 cup cornmeal
1½ cups all-purpose flour
½ cup slivered almonds, chopped
3 ounces white baking chocolate with cocoa butter, chopped
2 teaspoons finely shredded orange peel
5 ounces white baking chocolate with cocoa butter, coarsely chopped
1 tablespoon shortening
½ cup white jimmies or coarse sugar (optional)

1. Preheat oven to 375°F. In a large mixing bowl beat butter with a mixer on medium to high for 30 seconds. Add granulated sugar and baking powder. Beat until combined, scraping sides of bowl occasionally. Beat in egg and vanilla until combined. Beat in cornmeal. Beat in as much of the flour as you can with the mixer. Using a wooden spoon, stir in any remaining flour, the almonds, 3 ounces chopped white chocolate, and orange peel.
2. Divide dough into three portions. Shape each portion into an 8-inch log. Place logs about 4 inches apart on an ungreased large cookie sheet; flatten slightly. Bake about 20 minutes or until a wooden toothpick inserted near the centers comes out clean. Cool on cookie sheet for 1 hour.
3. Preheat oven to 325°F. Using a serrated knife, cut each log diagonally into ½-inch slices. Place slices on an ungreased cookie sheet. Bake for 8 minutes. Carefully turn slices over and bake for 8 to 10 minutes more or until lightly browned. Transfer to wire racks; cool for 1 hour.
4. In a small heavy saucepan stir 5 ounces white chocolate and shortening over low heat until melted and smooth. Dip tops of cookies in melted white chocolate and sprinkle immediately with white jimmies. Place cookies on waxed paper; let stand until white chocolate is set.

PER SERVING *108 cal., 6 g fat (3 g sat. fat), 14 mg chol., 47 mg sodium, 12 g carb., 0 g fiber, 1 g pro.*

WHITE CHOCOLATE,
CORNMEAL, AND
ALMOND MINI
BISCOTTI

LOVELY LEMON CRINKLES

Lovely Lemon Crinkles

PREP 25 minutes
BAKE 7 minutes at 375°F
MAKES 36 servings

1 15.25-ounce package lemon cake mix (for moist cake)
2 eggs
⅓ cup all-purpose flour
⅓ cup lemon-infused olive oil
2 tablespoons finely shredded lemon peel
2 tablespoons lemon juice
1 teaspoon lemon extract
½ teaspoon vanilla
   Granulated sugar
   Powdered sugar

1. Preheat oven to 375°F. Line a cookie sheet with parchment paper; set aside. In a large bowl stir together cake mix, eggs, flour, oil, lemon peel, lemon juice, lemon extract, and vanilla until combined. (Dough will be soft.)
2. Place granulated sugar in one bowl and powdered sugar in another bowl. For each cookie, drop 1 tablespoon of the dough into the granulated sugar; toss to coat with sugar (dough will have a soft ball shape). Drop ball in the powdered sugar to coat. Place balls 2 inches apart on the prepared cookie sheet.
3. Bake for 7 to 9 minutes or until edges are light brown. Cool on cookie sheet for 2 minutes. Transfer cookies to a wire rack; cool.

PER SERVING 86 cal., 3 g fat (1 g sat. fat), 10 mg chol., 82 mg sodium, 14 g carb., 0 g fiber, 1 g pro.

Giant Nutmeg Cookies

PREP 30 minutes
BAKE 13 minutes at 350°F
MAKES 24 servings

1½ cups shortening
2 cups sugar
2 tablespoons grated whole nutmeg or 1 tablespoon ground nutmeg
2 teaspoons baking soda
1 teaspoon ground cinnamon
¼ teaspoon salt

2 eggs
½ cup molasses
4½ cups all-purpose flour
⅓ cup sugar
1 teaspoon grated whole nutmeg
or ½ teaspoon ground nutmeg

1. Preheat oven to 350°F. In a large mixing bowl beat shortening with a mixer on medium to high for 30 seconds. Add the 2 cups sugar, the 2 tablespoons nutmeg, baking soda, cinnamon, and salt. Beat until combined, scraping sides of bowl occasionally. Beat in eggs and molasses until combined. Beat in as much of the flour as you can with the mixer. Using a wooden spoon, stir in any remaining flour.
2. In a small bowl stir together the ⅓ cup sugar and the 1 teaspoon nutmeg. Using a ¼-cup measure or cookie scoop, shape dough into 2-inch balls. Roll balls in sugar mixture to coat. Place balls 2½ inches apart on an ungreased cookie sheet.
3. Bake for 13 minutes or until tops are cracked and edges are firm (do not overbake). Cool on cookie sheet for 2 minutes. Transfer cookies to a wire rack; cool.

PER SERVING *303 cal., 14 g fat (4 g sat. fat), 16 mg chol., 139 mg sodium, 43 g carb., 1 g fiber, 3 g pro.*

Pomegranate-Raspberry Bars

PREP **20 minutes**
BAKE **44 minutes at 350°F**
MAKES **32 servings**

Nonstick cooking spray
1½ cups all-purpose flour
⅓ cup powdered sugar
¾ cup butter, softened
6 cups frozen raspberries
⅔ cup pomegranate juice
¼ cup lemon juice
¾ cup granulated sugar
⅓ cup cornstarch
¼ teaspoon salt
4 eggs, lightly beaten
Pomegranate seeds (optional)

1. Preheat oven to 350°F. Line a 13×9×2-inch baking pan with foil, extending the foil over edges of pan. Coat foil with cooking spray; set aside.

2. For crust, in a large mixing bowl stir together flour and powdered sugar; add butter. Beat on low to medium just until pastry starts to cling (pastry may seem crumbly at first but will come together with continued beating). Press pastry evenly onto the bottom of the prepared baking pan. Bake for 14 minutes.
3. Meanwhile, for filling in a medium saucepan combine frozen raspberries and pomegranate juice. Cook over medium-high heat for 5 minutes or until most of the berries are softened. Pour fruit through a fine-mesh sieve, pressing berries with a spoon to release their juices. Measure 2 cups juice, adding more pomegranate juice if necessary. Stir in lemon juice.

4. In a medium bowl stir together granulated sugar, cornstarch, and salt. Stir in eggs until combined. Stir in juice. Pour filling evenly over hot crust.
5. Bake for 30 minutes or until edges begin to brown and center appears set (a knife test will not work with this filling). Cool in pan on a wire rack. If desired, cover and chill until serving time. Using the edges of the foil, lift uncut bars out of pan. Cut into bars. If desired, sprinkle with pomegranate seeds before serving. Store, covered, in the refrigerator.

PER SERVING *113 cal., 5 g fat (3 g sat. fat), 35 mg chol., 66 mg sodium, 16 g carb., 1 g fiber, 2 g pro.*

POMEGRANATE-RASPBERRY BARS

COCONUT CREAM PIE BARS

Coconut Cream Pie Bars

PREP 30 minutes
BAKE 40 minutes at 350°F
COOL 1 hour CHILL 3 hours
MAKES 36 servings

  2 cups all-purpose flour
  ¾ cup flaked coconut
  ½ cup powdered sugar
  1 teaspoon finely shredded lime peel
  1 cup butter, softened
  1 cup granulated sugar
  ¼ cup cornstarch
  ¼ teaspoon salt
  3 cups whole milk
  ⅔ cup cream of coconut*
  5 egg yolks, lightly beaten
 1¼ teaspoons coconut extract
  1 teaspoon vanilla
  1 cup whipped cream
  ¼ cup fresh coconut curls or coconut shards, toasted if desired (see tip, page 19)

1. Preheat oven to 350°F. Line a 13×9×2-inch baking pan with foil, extending the foil over edges of pan. Set aside.
2. For crust, in a large bowl stir together flour, the ¾ cup flaked coconut, powdered sugar, and lime peel. Add butter, stirring to combine.

(Mixture will be crumbly; keep stirring until it comes together.) Press evenly onto the bottom of the prepared baking pan. Bake for 20 minutes or until crust is light brown. Cool on a wire rack.
3. For filling, in a large saucepan stir together granulated sugar, cornstarch, and salt. Gradually stir in milk and cream of coconut. Cook and stir over medium-high heat until thickened and bubbly; reduce heat. Cook and stir for 2 minutes more. Remove from heat. Gradually stir about 1 cup of the hot mixture into egg yolks. Return egg yolk mixture to saucepan. Bring to a gentle boil, stirring constantly; reduce heat. Cook and stir for 2 minutes more. Remove from heat. Stir in coconut extract and vanilla. Pour warm filling over crust.
4. Bake for 20 minutes or until filling is set. Cool on a wire rack for 1 hour. Cover and chill for 3 to 6 hours before serving. Using the edges of the foil, lift uncut bars out of pan. Cut into bars. Garnish with whipped cream and coconut curls.
PER SERVING *197 cal., 12 g fat (8 g sat. fat), 57 mg chol., 92 mg sodium, 21 g carb., 1 g fiber, 2 g pro.*
***Tip** Look for cream of coconut among the drink mixers in liquor stores.

Milk Chocolate Truffle Brownies

PREP 25 minutes
BAKE 25 minutes at 325°F
MAKES 20 servings

     Nonstick cooking spray
  ⅔ cup all-purpose flour
  ½ teaspoon baking powder
  ½ teaspoon salt
  ½ cup butter
  ½ cup milk chocolate pieces
  3 ounces unsweetened chocolate, chopped
  1 cup sugar
 1½ teaspoons vanilla
  3 eggs
  1 4.63-ounce package (10 squares) truffle-filled milk chocolate squares

1. Preheat oven to 325°F. Line a 9×9×2-inch baking pan with foil, extending the foil over edges of pan. Coat foil with cooking spray; set pan aside. In a small bowl stir together flour, baking powder, and salt; set aside.
2. In a medium saucepan stir butter, milk chocolate pieces, and unsweetened chocolate over low heat until melted and smooth. Cool slightly. Stir in sugar and vanilla until combined. Add eggs, one at a time, beating with a wooden spoon after each addition. Stir in flour mixture just until combined. Pour batter into the prepared baking pan, spreading evenly. Bake for 25 minutes.
3. Break milk chocolate squares into irregular pieces. Sprinkle on warm brownies. Cool in pan on a wire rack. Using the edges of the foil, lift uncut brownies out of pan. Cut into bars.
PER SERVING *192 cal., 12 g fat (7 g sat. fat), 44 mg chol., 131 mg sodium, 22 g carb., 1 g fiber, 3 g pro.*

MILK CHOCOLATE
TRUFFLE BROWNIES

Scrumptious Candy

SHOW YOUR AFFECTION with handmade confections suited to the season. Fill and share gift boxes with an array of sweets—truffles, nougat, marshmallows, fudge, and turtles.

HOMEMADE
MARSHMALLOWS,
PAGE 120

DULCE DE LECHE
SNAPPERS

Dulce de Leche Snappers

PREP 30 minutes
BAKE 8 minutes at 350°F
MAKES 36 servings

½ cup butter, softened
½ cup granulated sugar
½ cup packed brown sugar
½ teaspoon baking powder
¼ teaspoon salt
1 egg
1½ teaspoons vanilla
2 cups all-purpose flour
2 cups pecan halves, walnut halves, and/or whole almonds (about 108)
¾ cup dulce de leche
Sea salt flakes (optional)

1. Preheat oven to 350°F. In a medium mixing bowl beat butter with a mixer on medium to high for 30 seconds. Add granulated sugar, brown sugar, baking powder, and the ¼ teaspoon salt. Beat until combined, scraping sides of bowl occasionally. Beat in egg and vanilla until combined. Beat in as much of the flour as you can with the mixer. Using a wooden spoon, stir in any remaining flour.
2. Shape dough into thirty-six 1-inch balls. On an ungreased cookie sheet arrange nuts in groups of three, each group 2 inches apart. Place each ball of dough on a nut cluster, with nuts peeking out beneath the ball. Flatten dough slightly.
3. Bake for 8 to 10 minutes or just until edges are firm. Cool on cookie sheet for 1 minute. While cookies are warm, spread each cookie with 1 teaspoon of the dulce de leche. If desired, sprinkle with sea salt. Transfer cookies to a wire rack; cool.

PER SERVING *131 cal., 7 g fat (2 g sat. fat), 14 mg chol., 55 mg sodium, 15 g carb., 1 g fiber, 2 g pro.*

Cherry-Walnut Balls

PREP 40 minutes   COOL 5 minutes
BAKE 18 minutes at 325°F
MAKES 48 servings

¼ cup coarsely chopped maraschino cherries

CHERRY-WALNUT BALLS

1 cup butter, softened
½ cup powdered sugar
½ teaspoon almond extract
½ teaspoon vanilla
2 cups all-purpose flour
¾ cup chopped walnuts, toasted (see tip, page 19)
Powdered sugar (optional)

1. Preheat oven to 325°F. Drain maraschino cherries on paper towels; pat dry to remove excess liquid. Set cherries aside.
2. In a large mixing bowl beat butter with a mixer on medium to high for 30 seconds. Beat in the ½ cup powdered sugar, almond extract, and vanilla until combined, scraping sides of bowl occasionally. Beat in as much flour as you can with the mixer. Stir in any remaining flour, the nuts, and cherries with a wooden spoon.
3. Shape dough into 1-inch balls. Place 2 inches apart on ungreased cookie sheets. Bake for 18 to 20 minutes or until bottoms are lightly brown. Cool 5 minutes on cookie sheets on wire racks. Roll warm balls in powdered sugar to coat. Transfer balls to wire racks and cool completely.
4. If desired, roll cooled balls in additional powdered sugar before serving.

PER SERVING *74 cal., 5 g fat, 10 mg chol., 34 mg sodium, 6 g carb., 0 g fiber, 1 g pro.*

Cheesecake Pops

PREP 1 hour 30 minutes
BAKE 40 minutes at 350°F
COOL 15 minutes + 2 hours
CHILL 4 hours
FREEZE 1 hour 30 minutes
STAND 30 minutes
MAKES 50 servings

 3 8-ounce packages cream cheese, softened
 1 cup granulated sugar
 ¼ cup milk
 2 tablespoons all-purpose flour
 1 teaspoon vanilla bean paste or vanilla
 3 eggs, lightly beaten
 12 ounces chopped vanilla- or chocolate-flavor candy coating or other candy coating disks*
 12 ounces chopped semisweet, dark, or white baking chocolate; chopped vanilla- or chocolate-flavor candy coating; or other candy coating disks*
 50 lollipop sticks
 Decorations, such as shredded coconut, chopped toasted nuts, crushed candies, chopped chocolate, miniature chocolate pieces, chocolate-covered coffee beans, assorted sprinkles, or colored sugars

1. Preheat oven to 350°F. Line the sides of a 9-inch springform pan with waxed paper. Grease waxed paper; set pan aside.
2. In a large mixing bowl beat cream cheese, granulated sugar, milk, flour, and vanilla with a mixer on medium until combined. Stir in eggs. Pour batter into the prepared pan, spreading evenly. Bake for 40 to 50 minutes or until a 2½-inch area around edges appears set when gently shaken. Cool in pan on a wire rack for 15 minutes. Loosen waxed paper from sides of pan. Cool cheesecake completely on wire rack. Cover and chill for at least 4 hours. Remove waxed paper.

3. Line a baking sheet with waxed paper. Using a small ice cream scoop or tablespoon measure, scoop cooled cheesecake into 1½-inch mounds and drop onto prepared baking sheet. Roll mounds into smooth balls, moistening hands lightly with water if necessary. (If mounds are too sticky to handle easily, freeze for 15 minutes before rolling into balls.) Freeze for 30 minutes.
4. In a medium microwave-safe bowl heat candy coating and chocolate on 50% power for 4 to 5 minutes or until melted, stirring twice. For each cheesecake pop, dip one end of a lollipop stick into melted coating then insert the end into a cheesecake ball (to help balls stay on the sticks). Freeze for 1 hour or until firm.
5. Working in small batches, dip cheesecake pops into melted coating, spooning coating over balls and allowing excess to drip off. (If coating becomes too thick, heat on 50% power for 1 minute or until spooning consistency.) Sprinkle pops with decorations. Place on waxed paper. Let stand until coating is set.
6. Store in the refrigerator up to 3 days or freeze up to 1 month. If frozen, let stand at room temperature for 30 minutes before serving.
PER SERVING *151 cal., 10 g fat (6 g sat. fat), 26 mg chol., 49 mg sodium, 15 g carb., 1 g fiber, 2 g pro.*

Chocolate-Peppermint Pops Prepare as directed, except stir 1 cup miniature semisweet chocolate pieces and 1 teaspoon peppermint extract into cheesecake batter. To decorate pops, coat cheesecake balls with a mixture of melted chocolate-flavor candy coating and semisweet chocolate. Sprinkle with crushed candy canes or red and white sprinkles. If desired, drizzle with melted vanilla-flavor candy coating.

Pumpkin Pie Pops Prepare as directed, except in Step 2 omit one 8-ounce package cream cheese and the milk. Reduce granulated sugar to ½ cup and add ½ cup packed brown sugar. Beat in 1 cup canned pumpkin and ½ teaspoon pumpkin pie spice with the cream cheese. To decorate pops, microwave two 11-ounce packages butterscotch-flavor pieces and 1 teaspoon shortening until melted; coat cheesecake balls with butterscotch mixture. Sprinkle with crushed graham crackers and chopped toasted walnuts.
Almond Mocha Pops Prepare as directed, except in Step 2 omit the milk. Stir 1 cup milk chocolate or dark chocolate pieces, ¼ cup brewed coffee, and ½ to 1 teaspoon almond extract into cheesecake batter. To decorate pops, coat cheesecake balls with melted chocolate-flavor candy coating or a mixture of melted chocolate-flavor candy coating and dark chocolate. Sprinkle with whole or chopped chocolate-covered coffee beans or chopped toasted almonds.
Citrus Pops Prepare as directed, except in Step 2 omit the milk and vanilla. Stir 1 teaspoon finely shredded orange, lemon, and/or lime peel and ¼ cup orange juice into cheesecake batter. To decorate pops, coat cheesecake balls with melted white candy coating disks or a mixture of melted white candy coating disks and white baking chocolate. Sprinkle with crushed lemon drops, chocolate sprinkles, or red sprinkles.
* Look for colored candy-coating disks at hobby or crafts stores in the cake decorating department.

**NO-BAKE WHITE
CHOCOLATE-ALMOND
BUTTER BALLS**

No-Bake White Chocolate-Almond Butter Balls

PREP 30 minutes CHILL 50 minutes
MAKES 36 servings

- 1 cup almond butter
- ¼ cup butter, softened
- 1 cup powdered sugar
- 2 tablespoons unsweetened cocoa powder
- 2 cups crisp rice cereal
- 8 ounces white baking chocolate with cocoa butter, chopped
- 4 ounces vanilla-flavor candy coating
- 2 teaspoons shortening
- 2 ounces white baking chocolate with cocoa butter, chopped

1. Line a large cookie sheet with parchment paper; set aside. In a large mixing bowl beat almond butter and butter with a mixer on medium to high for 30 seconds. Gradually add powdered sugar and cocoa powder, beating until combined. Stir in rice cereal.
2. Using buttered hands, shape dough into 1-inch balls. Place balls on the prepared cookie sheet. Chill for 30 minutes.
3. In a small heavy saucepan stir 8 ounces white chocolate, candy coating, and shortening over low heat until melted and smooth.
4. Line another large cookie sheet or tray with waxed paper. Using a fork, dip chilled balls, one at a time, into melted white chocolate mixture, allowing excess to drip back into pan.* Place on the prepared cookie sheet or tray. Chill about 20 minutes or until firm.
5. Place 2 ounces chopped white chocolate in a small microwave-safe bowl. Microwave on 50% power for 1½ to 2 minutes or until chocolate is melted and smooth, stirring twice. Drizzle melted white chocolate over balls.
PER SERVING *137 cal., 9 g fat (4 g sat. fat), 5 mg chol., 41 mg sodium, 13 g carb., 1 g fiber, 2 g pro.*
*Tip If the coating mixture in the pan becomes too shallow for dipping, transfer it to a 1-cup glass measure cup or a custard cup to dip the last few balls.

Pumpkin-Gingerbread Truffles

PREP 45 minutes CHILL 2 hours
FREEZE 15 minutes
MAKES 30 servings

- 5 ounces bittersweet chocolate, chopped
- 5 ounces semisweet chocolate, chopped
- ½ cup finely crushed gingersnaps
- 1 3-ounce package cream cheese, softened
- ⅓ cup canned pumpkin
- 1 tablespoon powdered sugar
- ½ teaspoon finely shredded orange peel
- ⅛ teaspoon ground cinnamon
  Dash kosher salt
- 1 tablespoon unsweetened cocoa powder or finely crushed gingersnaps

1. In a small bowl combine bittersweet chocolate and semisweet chocolate. Place ½ cup of the chocolate mixture in a small saucepan; stir over medium-low heat until melted and smooth. Transfer to a medium bowl. Stir in ½ cup crushed gingersnaps, the cream cheese, pumpkin, powdered sugar, orange peel, cinnamon, and salt. Cover and chill for 1½ hours or until firm.
2. Divide mixture into 30 portions, using about 1 rounded teaspoon for each truffle. Shape each portion into a ball. Freeze for 15 minutes.
3. Meanwhile, line a baking sheet with waxed paper or parchment paper. In a medium saucepan heat and stir the remaining chocolate mixture over medium-low heat until melted and smooth.
4. Use a fork to dip frozen truffles, one at a time, into melted chocolate,* allowing excess to drip off. Place truffles on the prepared baking sheet. Immediately sprinkle with the cocoa powder or crushed gingersnaps. Chill about 30 minutes or until set.
PER SERVING *68 cal., 4 g fat (3 g sat. fat), 3 mg chol., 28 mg sodium, 8 g carb., 1 g fiber, 1 g pro.*
*Tip If the melted chocolate hardens slightly while dipping the truffles, reheat over medium-low heat until it is melted and smooth.

Easy Creamy Cranberry Fudge

PREP 20 minutes CHILL 2 hours
MAKES 64 servings

  Butter
- 3 cups white baking pieces
- 1 14-ounce can sweetened condensed milk
- ¾ cup dried cranberries, snipped
- ½ cup coarsely chopped pistachio nuts
- 2 teaspoons finely shredded orange peel
- 1 teaspoon vanilla

1. Line an 8×8×2-inch baking pan with foil, extending the foil over edges of pan. Butter foil; set pan aside.
2. In a 2-quart heavy saucepan stir baking pieces and condensed milk over low heat just until baking pieces are melted and smooth. Remove saucepan from heat. Stir in ½ cup of the dried cranberries, 6 tablespoons of the pistachios, orange peel, and vanilla.
3. Spread fudge evenly in the prepared pan. Top with the remaining dried cranberries and pistachios. Cover and chill for 2 hours or until firm.
4. Using the edges of the foil, lift fudge out of pan. Cut into 64 squares.
PER SERVING *70 cal., 4 g fat (3 g sat. fat), 5 mg chol., 19 mg sodium, 9 g carb., 0 g fiber, 1 g pro.*

EASY CREAMY CRANBERRY FUDGE

Homemade Marshmallows

(photo page 112)

PREP 30 minutes COOK 12 minutes
CHILL 5 hours MAKES 80 servings

  Nonstick cooking spray
 2 envelopes unflavored gelatin
  (4¼ teaspoons)
 ¾ cup cold water
 2 cups granulated sugar
 ⅔ cup light-color corn syrup
 ⅓ cup refrigerated egg white
  product* or 2 pasteurized liquid
  egg whites
 1 tablespoon vanilla
 ¼ teaspoon salt
 ⅔ cup powdered sugar
 3 tablespoons cornstarch
  Cocoa powder (optional)

1. Line a 13×9×2-inch baking pan with plastic wrap or line bottom of pan with waxed paper or parchment paper. Coat the plastic or paper with nonstick cooking spray; set pan aside.
2. In a large metal or heatproof bowl sprinkle gelatin over ½ cup of the cold water; set aside.
3. In a 2-quart heavy saucepan stir together remaining ¼ cup water, 1¾ cups of the sugar, and the corn syrup until combined. Bring to boiling over medium-high heat. Clip a candy thermometer to the side of the saucepan. Cook, without stirring, over medium-high heat until thermometer registers 260°F, hard-ball stage (12 to 15 minutes total). Remove from heat; pour over gelatin mixture in bowl and stir well to combine (mixture will foam and bubble up in the bowl).
4. Meanwhile, in a large clean mixing bowl beat the egg whites, vanilla, and salt with a mixer on high until foamy. Gradually add the remaining ¼ cup sugar, 1 tablespoon at a time, until stiff peaks form (tips stand straight). With the mixer running on high, gradually add gelatin mixture to egg white mixture, beating for 5 to 7 minutes or until thick (the consistency of thick, pourable cake batter). Quickly and gently spread marshmallow into prepared pan. Coat another piece of plastic wrap with nonstick

coating; place, coated side down, over marshmallow in pan. Chill at least 5 hours or until firm.
5. In a small bowl combine powdered sugar and cornstarch; evenly sprinkle about ¼ of the mixture onto a large cutting board. Remove plastic wrap from top of marshmallow. Loosen sides of marshmallow if necessary and carefully invert onto the cutting board. Remove plastic wrap or paper. Sprinkle top with some of the remaining powdered sugar mixture. Cut marshmallow into about 1-inch squares. Place squares, about one-third at a time, in a large resealable plastic bag. Add remaining powdered sugar mixture; seal bag and toss to coat all sides of marshmallows. If desired, use a stencil to dust cocoa powder over marshmallows.
6. Store marshmallows between sheets of waxed paper or parchment paper in an airtight container in the refrigerator up to 1 week or in the freezer up to 1 month.

PER SERVING *38 cal., 0 g fat, 0 mg chol., 20 mg sodium, 9 g carb., 0 g fiber, 0 g pro.*
* Be sure to use a product that is just egg whites.

Orange Cream Marshmallows
Prepare as above, except stir 1 envelope unsweetened orange-flavor soft drink mix into the egg whites with the vanilla.

Lemon-Pistachio Nougat

PREP 1 hour COOK 35 minutes
STAND 1 hour MAKES 24 servings

  Butter
  Cornstarch
 1½ cups sugar
 1 cup light-color corn syrup
 ½ cup water
 2 egg whites
 1 teaspoon vanilla
 1½ teaspoons finely shredded lemon
  peel
 ¾ cup chopped pistachio nuts
  Nonstick cooking spray
  Powdered sugar

1. Line a 9×5×3-inch loaf pan with foil, extending foil over the edges of the pan. Butter foil; sprinkle with a small amount of cornstarch. Set pan aside.

2. In a heavy 2-quart saucepan add sugar, corn syrup, and the water. Stir once just to moisten the sugar. Clip a candy thermometer to side of pan. Place over medium heat and bring to boiling without stirring. Continue boiling at a moderate, steady rate until thermometer registers 295°F, hard-crack stage (35 to 40 minutes). Adjust heat as necessary to maintain a steady boil.
3. Remove saucepan from heat. Remove thermometer. In a large mixing bowl* beat egg whites with a mixer on medium until stiff peaks form (tips stand straight). Gradually pour hot syrup in a thin stream over egg whites, beating with the mixer on medium to high. (Add syrup slowly without stopping to ensure proper blending, do not scrape down the sides.)
4. Add vanilla. Continue beating on high until candy becomes very thick and less glossy (5 to 6 minutes). When beaters are lifted, candy should fall in a ribbon, mound on itself, then slowly meld into candy in bowl.
5. Immediately stir in lemon peel and pistachio nuts. Coat a rubber spatula with nonstick spray. Use the spatula to quickly spoon nougat into the prepared pan. Let stand 1 hour. When nougat is firm, use foil to lift it out of pan. Place on cutting board. Coat a knife with nonstick spray. Cut into 2½×¾-inch pieces (24 pieces). Lightly coat pieces in powdered sugar. Wrap each piece in plastic wrap. Store in an airtight container at room temperature for up to 2 weeks.

PER SERVING *121 cal., 2 g fat (1 g sat. fat), 1 mg chol., 18 mg sodium, 26 g carb., 0 g fiber, 1 g pro.*
*Tip If using a hand mixer, use a bowl with a rubberized bottom or place a damp kitchen towel or paper towel under the mixing bowl to keep it in place so your hands are free to drizzle in the candy mixture while beating the egg whites.

LEMON-PISTACHIO
NOUGAT

SWEET PARTY MIX.
PAGE 129

HAPPY HOLIDAYS

PB AND J BANANA
BREAD, PAGE 125

SPEARMINT DIPS,
PAGE 126

To:

From:

SPICY-LIME
PISTACHIO NUTS.
PAGE 131

BITTERSWEET
CHOCOLATE BISCOTTI,
PAGE 126

To:
From:

Giving and Gratitude

A PRETTILY PACKAGED homemade treats show thoughtfulness and caring. These food gifts—both sweet and savory—are a lovely way to spread cheer to friends, neighbors, co-workers, teachers, and holiday-party hosts.

PB AND J
BANANA BREAD

PB and J Banana Bread

PREP 25 minutes
BAKE 1 hour 10 minutes at 350°F
COOL 10 minutes
MAKES 16 servings

2 cups all-purpose flour
1½ teaspoons baking powder
½ teaspoon baking soda
½ teaspoon ground cinnamon
¼ teaspoon salt
¼ teaspoon ground nutmeg
⅛ teaspoon ground ginger
2 eggs, lightly beaten
1½ cups mashed ripe bananas
 (4 to 5 medium)
1 cup sugar
½ cup vegetable oil or melted butter
¼ cup creamy peanut butter
¼ cup chopped peanuts
⅓ cup strawberry preserves
1 recipe Streusel-Nut Topping
 (optional)

1. Preheat oven to 350°F. Grease the bottom and ½ inch up the sides of a 9×5×3-inch loaf pan; set aside. In a large bowl stir together flour, baking powder, baking soda, cinnamon, salt, nutmeg, and ginger. Make a well in the center of flour mixture; set aside.
2. In a medium bowl combine eggs, mashed bananas, sugar, oil, and peanut butter. Add egg mixture all at once to flour mixture. Stir just until moistened (batter should be lumpy). Fold in peanuts. Spoon batter into the prepared loaf pan, spreading evenly. Drizzle with ¼ cup of the strawberry preserves; swirl slightly to marble. If desired, sprinkle with Streusel-Nut Topping.
3. Bake for 70 minutes or until a wooden toothpick inserted near the center comes out clean. If necessary to prevent overbrowning, cover loosely with foil for the last 15 minutes of baking. Cool in pan on a wire rack for 10 minutes. Remove from pan. Cool completely on wire rack. Wrap and store overnight.
4. In a small microwave-safe bowl heat the remaining strawberry preserves on high for 15 to 20 seconds or until melted, snipping any large pieces of fruit. Drizzle melted preserves over the top of bread before slicing.
PER SERVING *213 cal., 9 g fat (1 g sat. fat), 23 mg chol., 108 mg sodium, 32 g carb., 1 g fiber, 3 g pro.*

Streusel-Nut Topping In a small bowl combine 3 tablespoons brown sugar and 2 tablespoons all-purpose flour. Using a pastry blender, cut in 4 teaspoons butter until mixture resembles coarse crumbs. Stir in ¼ cup chopped dry-roasted peanuts.
To make three small loaves In Step 1 grease three 5¾×3×2-inch disposable mini loaf pans. In Step 2 divide the batter evenly between the three loaf pans. In Step 3 bake loaves for 35 to 45 minutes or until a toothpick inserted near the center of loaves comes out clean. Do not remove loaves from the pan. When completely cool, secure lids on the pans and tie with a ribbon.

Browned Butter and Oatmeal Crisps

PREP 35 minutes
BAKE 10 minutes at 350°F
MAKES 42 servings

¾ cup butter
1¾ cups quick-cooking rolled oats
¾ cup sugar
¾ cup all-purpose flour
½ teaspoon baking powder
¼ cup dark-color corn syrup
¼ cup whipping cream

1. In a small saucepan stir butter over medium heat until melted. Cook until butter turns light golden brown, stirring occasionally. Remove from heat.
2. Preheat oven to 350°F. Line a large cookie sheet with foil; set aside. In a large bowl stir together oats, sugar, flour, and baking powder. In a small bowl combine browned butter, corn syrup, and whipping cream. Add butter mixture to oat mixture, stirring to combine.
3. Drop dough by rounded teaspoons 3 inches apart onto the prepared cookie sheet. Bake for 10 minutes or until edges are golden and centers are bubbly. Cool crisps on cookie sheet. Carefully lift edges of crisps; peel cookies off foil.
PER SERVING *74 cal., 4 g fat (2 g sat. fat), 11 mg chol., 38 mg sodium, 9 g carb., 0 g fiber, 1 g pro.*
To wrap for giving Punch two small holes through both layers of waxed paper sandwich bags. Place cookies in bags, tie closed using bakers twine or decorative ribbon.

BROWNED BUTTER AND OATMEAL CRISPS

Bittersweet Chocolate Biscotti

PREP 25 minutes BAKE 20 minutes at 375°F / 15 minutes at 325°F
COOL 1 hour 45 minutes
MAKES 24 servings

⅓ cup butter, softened
⅔ cup packed brown sugar
2 teaspoons baking powder
½ teaspoon salt
2 eggs
¼ cup unsweetened cocoa powder
1⅔ cups all-purpose flour
1 cup toasted hazelnuts (filberts), chopped*
4 ounces bittersweet chocolate, chopped
6 ounces special dark chocolate or bittersweet chocolate, chopped (optional)
2 teaspoons shortening (optional)

1. Preheat oven to 375°F. Grease a cookie sheet; set aside. In a large mixing bowl beat butter with a mixer on medium to high for 30 seconds. Add brown sugar, baking powder, and salt. Beat until combined, scraping sides of bowl occasionally. Beat in eggs and cocoa powder until combined. Beat in as much of the flour as you can with the mixer. Using a wooden spoon, stir in any remaining flour, the hazelnuts, and the 4 ounces bittersweet chocolate.

BITTERSWEET CHOCOLATE BISCOTTI

2. Divide dough in half. Shape each half into a 9-inch log. Place logs 4 inches apart on the prepared cookie sheet; slightly flatten each log to about 2 inches wide.

3. Bake for 20 to 25 minutes or until a wooden toothpick inserted near centers comes out clean. Cool on cookie sheet for 45 minutes.

4. Preheat oven to 325°F. Using a serrated knife, cut each loaf diagonally into ½-inch slices. Place slices on an ungreased cookie sheet.

5. Bake for 8 minutes. Carefully turn slices over and bake for 7 to 9 minutes more or until biscotti are dry and crisp. Transfer to wire racks; cool for 1 hour.

6. If desired, in a small microwave-safe bowl heat 6 ounces dark chocolate and shortening on medium for 1 to 2 minutes or until melted, stirring twice. Dip one long side of each biscotti into melted chocolate, letting excess drip back into bowl. Place biscotti on waxed paper; let stand until chocolate is set.

PER SERVING *140 cal., 8 g fat (3 g sat. fat), 22 mg chol., 120 mg sodium, 17 g carb., 1 g fiber, 3 g pro.*

*Tip To toast hazelnuts, preheat oven to 375°F. Spread nuts in a single layer in a shallow baking pan. Bake for 4 to 5 minutes or until light golden brown, stirring once or twice. Wrap warm nuts in a clean kitchen towel, rub to remove any loose skins; cool completely. Chop nuts and set aside.

To wrap as a gift Write recipient's name or a greeting on self-adhesive stickers. Place stickers on the center of small decorative bags. Fill the bags with biscotti.

Spearmint Dips

PREP 55 minutes CHILL 1 hour
BAKE 7 minutes at 375°F
MAKES 96 servings

1 cup butter, softened
1 cup granulated sugar
1 teaspoon baking powder
¼ teaspoon salt
1 egg
1 teaspoon vanilla
2¼ cups all-purpose flour
½ teaspoon mint extract
   Green paste food coloring
9 ounces white baking chocolate with cocoa butter, chopped

2 teaspoons shortening
   Red, white, and/or green jimmies, sprinkles, or nonpareils (optional)

1. In a large mixing bowl beat butter with a mixer on medium to high for 30 seconds. Add granulated sugar, baking powder, and salt. Beat until combined, scraping sides of bowl occasionally. Beat in egg and vanilla until combined. Beat in as much of the flour as you can with the mixer. Using a wooden spoon, stir in remaining flour.

2. Divide dough in half. Leave one portion plain. Stir mint extract into remaining portion and add enough food coloring to tint dough green. Divide each portion of dough in half. Cover and chill about 1 hour or until dough is easy to handle.

3. Preheat oven to 375°F. On waxed paper, roll a plain portion of dough into a 9×6-inch rectangle. On a floured surface, roll a green portion into a 9×6-inch rectangle. Use waxed paper to invert plain dough rectangle on the green dough rectangle; peel off waxed paper. If necessary, press edges to align them. Cut each stacked rectangle into twenty-four 1½-inch squares. Cut each square in half diagonally to make 48 triangles. Repeat with remaining dough portions.

4. Place triangles 1 inch apart on an ungreased cookie sheet. Bake for 7 to 8 minutes or until edges are firm and bottoms are light brown. Transfer cookies to wire racks; cool.

5. In a small saucepan stir white chocolate and shortening over low heat until melted. Dip half of each cookie into the white chocolate mixture, allowing excess to drip back into saucepan. Place cookies on trays lined with waxed paper. If desired, sprinkle dipped portions with jimmies. Chill until white chocolate is set.

PER SERVING *52 cal., 3 g fat (2 g sat. fat), 8 mg chol., 31 mg sodium, 6 g carb., 0 g fiber, 1 g pro.*

To package for giving Cut parchment to fit macaron boxes (available online or at crafts stores). Lay cookies inside the box. Using a snowflake punch, cut several snowflakes and attach to box with glue dots. Tie box with a ribbon.

SPEARMINT
DIPS

HOMEMADE COCONUT
GRANOLA

Homemade Coconut Granola

PREP 20 minutes BAKE 20 minutes at 300°F /25 minutes at 350°F
MAKES 34 servings

2½ cups rolled oats
1½ cups flaked or shredded coconut
¼ cup shelled sunflower seeds
¼ cup sesame seeds
¼ cup butter
¼ cup packed brown sugar
¼ cup honey or agave nectar
1 teaspoon vanilla
½ teaspoon almond extract
½ cup toasted wheat germ
1 cup dried cranberries and/or golden raisins

1. Preheat oven to 300°F. Lightly butter or grease bottom and sides of a large roasting pan. Evenly spread oatmeal, coconut, sunflower seeds, and sesame seeds in pan. Bake for 20 minutes, stirring twice.
2. Meanwhile, in a small saucepan combine butter, brown sugar, and honey. Stir constantly over medium heat until butter is melted and mixture is combined. Remove from heat. Stir in vanilla and almond extract.
3. Carefully remove roasting pan from oven; place on a wire cooling rack. Increase oven temperature to 350°F. Add wheat germ to oats. Pour warm brown sugar mixture over oats. With a large spoon or spatula, stir the granola until it is thoroughly coated with brown sugar mixture. Bake 5 minutes. Remove pan from oven; place on a wire cooling rack.
4. Stir cranberries and/or raisins into granola. With a spatula, firmly press granola in an even layer. Bake about 20 minutes more or until golden brown, stirring twice. Remove pan from oven and place on a wire cooling rack. With a spatula, remove the granola from pan (granola will be crumbly). Spread pieces on a large piece of foil. Cool completely.
5. Store in an airtight container up to 2 weeks.
PER SERVING *97 cal., 4 g fat (2 g sat. fat), 4 mg chol., 23 mg sodium, 15 g carb., 2 g fiber, 2 g pro.*
To package for giving Remove the lids from two deep aluminum foil

SWEET PARTY MIX

food containers. Trace the lid onto two 12×12 pieces of snowflake die cut paper; cut out and use glue dots to adhere to lid. Place jumbo size muffin cup liners in the containers and fill each with some of the granola. Attach tags to lids using snowflake brads. Secure lids on each container.

Sweet Party Mix

PREP 20 minutes
BAKE 20 minutes at 300°F
MAKES 36 servings

Nonstick cooking spray
4 cups bite-size corn square cereal
3 cups bite-size rice square cereal
2 cups pretzel knots
⅔ cup sliced almonds
½ cup packed brown sugar
¼ cup butter
2 tablespoons light-color corn syrup
⅛ teaspoon baking soda
¾ cup dried cranberries, blueberries, and/or cherries

1. Preheat oven to 300°F. Lightly coat a large piece of foil with cooking spray; set aside. In a large roasting pan toss together corn cereal, rice cereal, pretzels, and almonds; set aside.
2. In a medium saucepan combine brown sugar, butter, and corn syrup. Cook and stir over medium heat just until mixture begins to bubble. Continue cooking at a moderate, steady rate, without stirring, for 5 minutes more. Remove saucepan from heat; stir in baking soda. Pour over cereal mixture; stir gently to coat.
3. Bake for 15 minutes; stir and bake 5 minutes more. Remove from oven; stir in dried fruit. Spread party mix on prepared foil to cool. Store in an airtight container.
PER SERVING *74 cal., 2 g fat (1 g sat. fat), 3 mg chol., 106 mg sodium, 13 g carb., 1 g fiber, 1 g pro.*
To package for giving Place paper nut cups in disposable foil muffin tins. Fill nut cups with the party mix. Secure muffin tin covers. Use glue dots to attach chipboard or wooden letters to the covers.

SPICY-LIME
PISTACHIO NUTS

Spicy-Lime Pistachio Nuts

PREP 10 minutes
BAKE 20 minutes at 325°F
STAND 2 hours MAKES 24 servings

¼ cup olive oil
2 tablespoons lime juice
1 tablespoon pure maple syrup
2 teaspoons kosher or sea salt
½ to 1 teaspoon crushed red pepper
6 cups roasted salted pistachio nuts, whole almonds, and/or cashews

1. Preheat oven to 325°F. In a large bowl combine olive oil, lime juice, maple syrup, salt, and crushed red pepper. Add nuts; stir to coat. Spread nut mixture onto two large rimmed baking sheets in a single layer.
2. Bake for 20 minutes or until nuts are toasted and appear dry, stirring occasionally. Spread nuts on a large sheet of foil; cool completely. Let stand 2 hours before serving. Store in an airtight container at room temperature up to 3 weeks.

PER SERVING *195 cal., 16 g fat (2 g sat. fat), 0 mg chol., 164 mg sodium, 9 g carb., 3 g fiber, 6 g pro.*

To package for giving Place colorful paper napkins inside small pails (available at crafts or party stores). Fill with nuts. Tie a small ornament and gift tag to the handle.

Peppermint Hot Cocoa Mix

START TO FINISH 10 minutes
MAKES 20 servings

3 cups nonfat dry milk powder
1½ cups unsweetened cocoa powder
¾ cup sugar
½ cup crushed peppermint candies (3 ounces)

1. In a large bowl stir together milk powder, cocoa powder, sugar, and crushed candy. Place mix in an airtight container and store at room temperature for up to 3 months.
2. To serve, shake contents of the container. For each serving, place 3 tablespoons of the mix in a 10-ounce mug and add 1 cup boiling water; mix well (candies will dissolve in about 2 minutes).

PER SERVING *139 cal., 1 g fat (0 g sat. fat), 4 mg chol., 99 mg sodium, 24 g carb., 0 g fiber, 8 g pro.*

Mocha Hot Cocoa Mix Prepare as directed, except omit the peppermint candies and add ¼ cup instant coffee crystals or instant espresso coffee powder.

To package for giving Fill glass jars with cocoa mix; adding crushed candies to top the mix. Tie ribbon around jar, securing a measuring spoon. Decorate an empty oatmeal containers or coffee tins with scrapbook. Place jars inside containers. Tie twine around containers, securing a gift tag. Include serving directions with each gift. Makes five 1-cup gifts.

PEPPERMINT HOT COCOA MIX

AZTEC HOT FUDGE
SAUCE

Aztec Hot Fudge Sauce

PREP 10 minutes SLOW COOK 3 hours
MAKES 6 half-pints

3 cups semisweet chocolate pieces
2⅔ cups sugar
4 5-ounce cans evaporated milk
1 cup butter, cut up
1 teaspoon instant espresso coffee powder
¼ teaspoon salt
⅛ teaspoon ground cinnamon
⅛ teaspoon cayenne pepper (optional)
2 tablespoons coffee liqueur

1. In a 3½- or 4-quart slow cooker combine chocolate pieces, sugar, evaporated milk, butter, coffee powder, salt, cinnamon, and, if desired, cayenne pepper.
2. Cover and cook on low-heat setting for 3 hours, stirring once halfway through cooking. Whisk until smooth. Stir in liqueur. Cool slightly.
3. Ladle sauce into sterilized half-pint canning jars. Seal and label. Store in the refrigerator up to 2 weeks.
4. To reheat sauce, spoon ¾ to 1 cup of the sauce into a 1-cup glass measuring cup. Microwave, uncovered, on high for 1 to 1½ minutes or until heated through, stirring once.
PER 2-TABLESPOON SERVING 149 cal., 8 g fat (5 g sat. fat), 14 mg chol., 61 mg sodium, 20 g carb., 1 g fiber, 1 g pro.
To package for giving Fill six half-pint glass jars with hot fudge sauce; secure lid. Place the glass jar inside a take-out soup container; secure lid. Rubber stamp a greeting or name to a small wooden spoon. Tie a narrow ribbon around the container, then tie the spoon to the top.

Bacon and Tomato Spread

PREP 30 minutes SLOW COOK 5 hours
MAKES Makes 5 or 6 (4-ounce) jars

1½ pounds bacon, cut into 1-inch pieces
1 cup chopped red onion (1 large)
4 cloves garlic, sliced
2 pounds roma tomatoes, peeled, seeded, and coarsely chopped (3 cups)*

1 cup packed brown sugar
½ cup cider vinegar
½ cup strong brewed coffee
¼ teaspoon crushed red pepper

1. In a large skillet cook bacon over medium heat until crisp. Using a slotted spoon, remove bacon and drain on paper towels, reserving 2 tablespoons drippings in skillet.
2. Add onion and garlic to the reserved drippings. Cook over medium heat until onion is tender and light brown, stirring occasionally.
3. Transfer onion mixture to a 5- to 6-quart slow cooker. Add bacon, tomatoes, brown sugar, vinegar, coffee, and crushed red pepper. Cook, uncovered, on high-heat setting for 5 to 6 hours or until most of the liquid is evaporated, stirring occasionally. Cool slightly.
4. Drain tomato mixture, reserving juice. Transfer tomato mixture to a food processor. Cover and process with several on/off pulses until finely chopped. If desired, add some of the reserved juice and process until spreading consistency.
5. Ladle tomato spread into sterilized 4-ounce canning jars. Seal and label. Store in the refrigerator up to 1 month.
PER 1-TABLESPOON SERVING 113 cal., 7 g fat (2 g sat. fat), 17 mg chol., 296 mg sodium, 7 g carb., 0 g fiber, 6 g pro.
*Tip To peel tomatoes, use a small sharp knife to cut a shallow X on the bottom of each tomato. Immerse tomatoes, in batches, in boiling water to cover. Blanch for 30 to 60 seconds or until tomato skins split open. Using a slotted spoon, transfer tomatoes to a large bowl of ice water. When cool enough to handle, use a knife or fingers to peel off skins.
To package for giving Cut jar lid toppers from scrapbook paper. Fill small jars with Bacon and Tomato Spread. Wrap ribbons around jars. Using glue dots, attach tags to lids.

BACON AND TOMATO SPREAD

MUSSELS WITH LEEKS AND
PANCETTA, PAGE 137

Celebrate the New Year

THE START OF SOMETHING new is always cause for celebration. This sophisticated food—from appetizers to main dishes, sides, and desserts—will help you ring in the coming year with style and great tastes.

BUTTERNUT-SAGE
CROSTINI WITH
RICOTTA AND
HAZELNUTS

Butternut-Sage Crostini with Ricotta and Hazelnuts

PREP **40 minutes**
ROAST **35 minutes at 375°F**
BAKE **9 minutes at 400°F**
MAKES **15 servings**

- 1 2-pound butternut squash
- ¾ cup whole-milk ricotta cheese
- 1 teaspoon finely shredded lemon peel
- ½ teaspoon cracked black pepper
- ¼ teaspoon salt
  Dash cayenne pepper
- 1 tablespoon slivered fresh sage leaves
- ⅔ cup hazelnuts, toasted and chopped (see tip, page 126)
- 2 tablespoons lemon juice
- 1 1-pound loaf baguette-style French bread
- ¼ cup extra virgin olive oil
  Fresh sage leaves (optional)

1. Preheat oven to 375°F. Line a baking sheet with parchment paper. Cut squash in half lengthwise; scoop out seeds. Place halves, cut sides down, on the prepared baking sheet. Roast squash for 35 to 40 minutes or until tender. Set aside to cool slightly. Increase oven temperature to 400°F.
2. Meanwhile, in a medium bowl stir together ricotta cheese, lemon peel, black pepper, salt, and cayenne pepper; set aside.
3. Scoop flesh from squash halves and transfer to a food processor. Add the 1 tablespoon slivered sage, ⅓ cup of the hazelnuts, and the lemon juice. Cover and process until smooth; set aside.
4. Slice baguette diagonally into ½-inch slices. (You should have about 30 slices.) On an extra-large baking sheet arrange baguette slices in a single layer. Brush slices lightly with half the olive oil. Bake for 5 to 6 minutes or until slices begin to brown. Turn baguette slices over; brush lightly with the remaining olive oil. Bake for 4 to 5 minutes more or until second sides begin to brown.
5. Thickly spread pureed butternut squash on baguette slices. Top with ricotta mixture. Sprinkle with the remaining ⅓ cup chopped hazelnuts.

Serve warm or at room temperature. If desired, garnish with whole sage leaves.
PER SERVING *108 cal., 4 g fat (1 g sat. fat), 3 mg chol., 139 mg sodium, 15 g carb., 1 g fiber, 4 g pro.*

Garlicky White Bean Dip

START TO FINISH **15 minutes**
MAKES **10 servings**

- 1 15-ounce can white beans, rinsed and drained
- 4 to 5 cloves garlic, sliced
- ¼ teaspoon salt
- ⅛ teaspoon black pepper
- ¼ to ⅓ cup olive oil
- ¼ cup chopped fresh basil
  Pinch crushed red pepper
- 1 teaspoon olive oil
  Assorted fresh vegetables
  Toasted baguette slices

1. In a food processor combine white beans, garlic, salt, and pepper. With machine running, drizzle in enough of the ¼ to ⅓ cup olive oil to desired consistency.
2. Stir in basil. Sprinkle with crushed red pepper and drizzle with 1 teaspoon olive oil. Serve with vegetables and/or baguette slices.
PER SERVING *92 cal., 6 g fat (1 g sat. fat), 0 mg chol., 164 mg sodium, 7 g carb., 2 g fiber, 3 g pro.*

Mussels with Leeks and Pancetta

PREP **20 minutes** COOK **13 minutes**
STAND **45 minutes**
MAKES **4 servings**

- 1 pound mussels in shells (about 30)
- 1 cup salt
- 3 ounces pancetta, chopped
- 3 medium leeks, sliced (1 cup)
- ½ teaspoon finely shredded orange peel
- ½ cup orange juice
- ½ cup dry white wine
- 2 to 3 tablespoons snipped fresh chives
  Crusty country bread (optional)

1. Scrub mussels under cold running water. Remove beards. In an 8-quart Dutch oven combine 4 quarts cold water and ⅓ cup of the salt; add mussels. Soak for 15 minutes; drain and rinse. Discard water. Repeat soaking, draining, and rinsing twice.
2. In a Dutch oven cook pancetta over medium heat until crisp. Using a slotted spoon, remove pancetta from Dutch oven; drain on paper towels. Drain fat from the Dutch oven, reserving 1 tablespoon. Return the 1 tablespoon fat to Dutch oven. Add leeks; cook and stir about 3 minutes or until tender.
3. Add orange peel, orange juice, and wine to Dutch oven. Bring to boiling. Add mussels to Dutch oven; reduce heat. Simmer, covered, for 5 to 7 minutes or until mussels open. Discard any mussels that do not open. Sprinkle with pancetta and chives. If desired, serve with crusty country bread.
PER SERVING *333 cal., 11 g fat (3 g sat. fat), 47 mg chol., 905 mg sodium, 33 g carb., 2 g fiber, 20 g pro.*

MUSSELS WITH LEEKS AND PANCETTA

Roast Beef with Mushroom-Fig Sauce

PREP 20 minutes
ROAST 1 hour 30 minutes at 325°F
STAND 15 minutes COOK 18 minutes
MAKES 8 servings

- 1 2- to 2½-pound beef eye round roast
- ½ teaspoon cracked black pepper
- ¼ teaspoon salt
- 1 tablespoon olive oil
- 8 ounces fresh cremini or button mushrooms, sliced
- 2 tablespoons sliced shallot or sweet onion
- ½ cup dry red wine or lower-sodium beef broth
- 1 tablespoon Dijon mustard
- 1 teaspoon snipped fresh rosemary or ½ teaspoon dried rosemary, crushed
- ¾ cup lower-sodium beef broth
- ½ cup chopped, stemmed dried figs
  Snipped fresh rosemary

1. Preheat oven to 325°F. Trim fat from meat. Sprinkle meat with the pepper and salt, rubbing in with your fingers.
2. Place meat on a rack in a shallow roasting pan. Insert an oven-going meat thermometer into center of roast. Roast, uncovered, for 1½ to 1¾ hours or until thermometer registers 135°F (it is not recommended to roast an eye round roast past medium-rare). Cover meat with foil and let stand for 15 minutes before slicing. Temperature of the meat after standing should be 145°F.
3. Meanwhile, for Mushroom-Fig Sauce, in a large skillet heat oil over medium heat. Add mushrooms and shallot to skillet. Cook over medium heat for 5 to 8 minutes or just until mushrooms are tender and lightly browned, stirring occasionally. Remove from heat and add wine to skillet. Return to heat and bring to boiling; boil gently, uncovered, about 3 minutes or until wine is reduced by about half. Whisk in mustard and the 1 teaspoon rosemary. Add broth and figs. Bring to boiling; boil gently, uncovered, about 10 minutes or until liquid is slightly thickened and reduced by about one-third.
4. Thinly slice meat and serve with Mushroom-Fig Sauce. Garnish with rosemary.

PER SERVING *243 cal., 10 g fat (4 g sat. fat), 46 mg chol., 226 mg sodium, 8 g carb., 1 g fiber, 26 g pro.*

Stuffed Pork Loin

PREP 55 minutes
ROAST 1 hour at 350°F
STAND 10 minutes
MAKES 8 servings

- 1 recipe Spinach and Apricot Stuffing
- 1 3-pound boneless pork top loin roast (single loin)
- 1 teaspoon snipped fresh thyme or ¼ teaspoon dried thyme, crushed
- ¼ teaspoon salt
- ¼ teaspoon black pepper
- 1 cup water
- ⅓ cup cold water
- 2 tablespoons flour
  Cracked black pepper (optional)
  Snipped fresh thyme sprigs (optional)

1. Prepare Spinach and Apricot Stuffing; set aside. Trim fat from pork. Butterfly the meat by making a lengthwise cut down the center of the meat, cutting to within ½ inch of under side; spread open. Place a knife in the V of the cut and cut horizontally to the cut surface and away from the center cut to within ½ inch of the opposite side. Cut on the other side of the V. Spread meat open. Cover the roast with plastic wrap. Working from center (thick part) to edges, pound with flat side of a meat mallet until meat is an even ½- to ¾-inches. Remove plastic wrap. Set meat aside.
2. Preheat oven to 350°F. Spread stuffing evenly on the meat. Roll meat

ROAST BEEF WITH MUSHROOM-FIG SAUCE

STUFFED PORK LOIN

into a spiral, starting from a short side. Tie roast in three or four places with heavy 100%-cotton kitchen string. Place roast on a rack in a shallow roasting pan. Sprinkle with thyme, salt, and pepper. Insert an oven-going meat thermometer into center of roast. Roast, uncovered, for 1 to 1½ hours or until thermometer registers 145°F, covering ends of meat after 45 minutes to prevent stuffing from drying out. Transfer roast to a serving platter. Cover loosely with foil; let stand while preparing gravy.

3. For pan gravy, add the 1 cup water to roasting pan. Use a wire whisk to stir and scrape up browned bits. In a small saucepan whisk together the ⅓ cup cold water and the flour. Whisk in pan juices. Cook and stir over medium heat until thickened and bubbly. Cook and stir 1 minute more. Season to taste with additional salt and black pepper. If desired, sprinkle gravy with cracked black pepper.

4. Remove string from pork roast; discard. Slice roast; serve with gravy. Top with snipped fresh thyme sprigs.

Spinach and Apricot Stuffing In a large stockpot cook 12 cups loosely packed fresh spinach in rapidly boiling water for 1 minute. Drain well, squeezing out excess liquid. Pat dry with paper towels. Using kitchen shears, coarsely snip spinach; set aside. In a large skillet cook ½ cup finely chopped shallots and 2 cloves minced garlic in 1 tablespoon hot olive oil for 3 minutes or until shallots are tender. Remove from heat. Cool for 5 minutes. Stir in spinach, 2 ounces chopped prosciutto, ½ cup snipped dried apricots, ⅓ cup chopped toasted pecans (see tip, page 19), and ½ cup shredded Gruyère or Swiss cheese.

PER SERVING *324 cal., 11 g fat (4 g sat. fat), 105 mg chol., 412 mg sodium, 19 g carb., 1 g fiber, 37 g pro.*

Coconut Squash Soup with Seared Scallops

START TO FINISH 1 hour 15 minutes
MAKES 4 servings

- 8 medium fresh or frozen sea scallops (8 to 9 ounces) Nonstick cooking spray
- 2 medium leeks, trimmed and thinly sliced
- 3 cloves garlic, minced
- 2 teaspoons grated fresh ginger
- 2 cups low-sodium vegetable broth
- 1 2-pound butternut squash, peeled and cut into 1-inch pieces (6 cups)
- 1 14-ounce can reduced-fat unsweetened coconut milk
- ⅛ teaspoon cayenne pepper
- ½ teaspoon ground coriander
- ⅛ teaspoon salt
- ⅛ teaspoon black pepper
- ¼ cup pumpkin seeds, toasted (pepitas) (see tip, page 19) (optional)
- 2 tablespoons snipped fresh cilantro
- 2 teaspoons finely shredded lime peel (optional)

1. Thaw scallops, if frozen. Rinse scallops and pat dry with paper towels; set aside.
2. Coat a large unheated saucepan with cooking spray; heat pan over medium heat. Add leeks. Cook for 3 minutes, stirring occasionally. Add garlic and ginger. Cook and stir for 1 minute more.
3. Add broth and squash to leeks. Bring to boiling; reduce heat. Simmer, covered, for 15 minutes or until squash is tender. Remove from heat and cool slightly.
4. Transfer squash mixture to a blender or food processor. Cover and blend or process until smooth. Return pureed squash to saucepan. Stir in coconut milk and cayenne pepper. Heat through over medium-low heat, stirring occasionally (do not boil).
5. In a small bowl combine coriander, salt, and black pepper. Sprinkle evenly over scallops. Coat a large nonstick skillet or an unheated indoor grill pan with cooking spray; heat over medium-high heat. Add scallops to grill pan or skillet. Cook for 3 to 4 minutes or until scallops are opaque, turning once halfway through cooking.
6. To serve, ladle soup into four serving bowls. Float two scallops on each serving of soup. Sprinkle with pumpkin seeds (if using), cilantro, and lime peel (if using).

PER SERVING *234 cal., 6 g fat (4 g sat. fat), 14 mg chol., 614 mg sodium, 39 g carb., 5 g fiber, 10 g pro.*

Roasted Root Vegetable and Wilted Romaine Salad

PREP 30 minutes BAKE 30 minutes at 375°F/ 30 minutes at 425°F
MAKES 12 servings

- 2 medium fresh beets (about 12 ounces)
- 8 tablespoons olive oil Salt and black pepper
- 1¾ pounds fresh carrots, turnips, and/or parsnips
- 4 medium shallots, peeled and quartered
- 2 tablespoons white wine vinegar
- 1 tablespoon snipped fresh thyme
- 1 teaspoon Dijon mustard
- 1 teaspoon honey
- 1 clove garlic, minced
- 8 cups torn romaine
- ½ cup pecan halves, toasted (see tip, page 19)
- ¼ cup chopped fresh flat-leaf parsley

ROASTED ROOT VEGETABLE AND WILTED ROMAINE SALAD

1. Preheat oven to 375°F. Wash and peel the beets; cut into 1-inch pieces. Place in a 2-quart baking dish. Toss with 1 tablespoon of the olive oil and the salt and pepper to taste. Cover dish tightly with foil and bake for 30 minutes.

2. Meanwhile, peel the carrots, turnips, and/or parsnips. Cut carrots and turnips into irregular 1-inch pieces. Cut parsnips into irregular ¾-inch pieces. Place in a 15×10×1-inch baking pan. Add shallots. Toss with 1 tablespoon of the olive oil. Sprinkle with additional salt and pepper.

3. Remove foil from dish with beets; stir beets gently. Increase oven temperature to 425°F. Return beets to oven and place pan with shallot mixture alongside beets. Roast both pans, uncovered, for 30 to 40 minutes or until tender.

4. Meanwhile, for dressing, in a screw-top jar combine the remaining 6 tablespoons olive oil, the white wine vinegar, thyme, mustard, honey, garlic, and additional salt and pepper to taste; cover and shake well.

5. To serve, in a large bowl toss the romaine with the dressing. Place on a platter. Top with the hot vegetables. Sprinkle pecans and parsley over all. Serve immediately.

PER SERVING *165 cal., 13 g fat (2 g sat. fat), 0 mg chol., 179 mg sodium, 13 g carb., 4 g fiber, 2 g pro.*

Toasted Sesame Green Beans with Teriyaki Glaze

PREP 20 minutes COOK 10 minutes
MAKES 8 servings

1½ pounds green beans, trimmed
  1 cup julienned carrots (2 medium) or packaged fresh julienned carrots
  ¾ cup chicken broth
  ¼ cup soy sauce
  ¼ cup hoisin sauce
  1 tablespoon cornstarch
  1 tablespoon toasted sesame oil
  3 tablespoons canola oil
  2 cups sliced fresh mushrooms
  1 tablespoon grated fresh ginger
  4 cloves garlic, minced

TOASTED SESAME GREEN BEANS WITH TERIYAKI GLAZE

  2 tablespoons snipped fresh basil
  1 tablespoon sesame seeds

1. Bring a large pot of salted water to boiling. Add green beans; return to boiling. Boil for 4 minutes. Add carrots; boil for 1 minute. Drain.

2. In a small bowl stir together chicken broth, soy sauce, hoisin sauce, cornstarch, and sesame oil; set aside.

3. In a large wok or an extra-large nonstick skillet heat canola oil over high heat. Add mushrooms, ginger, and garlic; cook and stir about 3 minutes

or until mushrooms are tender. Stir broth mixture and add to skillet; cook and stir about 1 minute or just until thickened and bubbly. Stir in green beans, carrots, and basil; heat through.

4. To serve, sprinkle with toasted sesame seeds.

PER SERVING *131 cal., 8 g fat (1 g sat. fat), 1 mg chol., 741 mg sodium, 14 g carb., 3 g fiber, 3 g pro.*

PARSNIP-POTATO MASH WITH LEEKS AND HAZELNUT BROWNED BUTTER

Parsnip-Potato Mash with Leeks and Hazelnut Browned Butter

PREP 20 minutes   COOK 30 minutes
MAKES 8 servings

  1 pound Yukon gold potatoes, peeled and coarse-chopped
 20 ounces parsnips, peeled and sliced (2 medium)
  6 tablespoons butter
  3 to 4 tablespoons whole milk
 ⅔ cup sliced leeks (white part only) (2 medium)
 ½ teaspoon salt
 ¼ teaspoon black pepper
  2 tablespoons snipped fresh parsley
 ¼ cup finely chopped hazelnuts (filberts), toasted (see tip, page 19)

1. In a Dutch oven cook the potatoes, covered, in a small amount of salted boiling water about 5 minutes. Add the parsnips; cook for 15 minutes or until potatoes and parsnips are tender. Drain well. Return potatoes and parsnips to Dutch oven; add 2 tablespoons of the butter. Mash with a potato masher or fork, adding whole milk as needed to keep the mash moist; keep warm.
2. Meanwhile, in a small saucepan cook leeks in 2 tablespoons of the butter about 7 minutes or until tender and just beginning to brown. Add salt and pepper. Stir leeks and parsley into the parsnip-potato mash.
3. For hazelnut Browned Butter, in the same saucepan melt the remaining 2 tablespoons butter over low heat. Continue heating until butter turns a light golden brown. Remove from heat; add the hazelnuts.
4. Gently heat and stir parsnip-potato mash over medium heat until heated through. Season to taste with additional salt and pepper. Transfer to a serving bowl. Top with Hazelnut Browned Butter.

PER SERVING *186 cal., 11 g fat (6 g sat. fat), 23 mg chol., 452 mg sodium, 20 g carb., 4 g fiber, 3 g pro.*

Chile-Corn Custards

PREP 35 minutes
ROAST 20 minutes at 425°F
STAND 20 minutes
BAKE 30 minutes at 325°F
MAKES 6 servings

  2 medium fresh poblano or Anaheim chile peppers (see tip, page 34)
  1 small red sweet pepper
  5 eggs, lightly beaten
 ¾ cup whipping cream
 1½ cups frozen whole kernel corn, thawed and well drained
 ¾ cup shredded Monterey Jack cheese with jalapeño peppers (3 ounces)
 ½ cup fine soft bread crumbs
  2 tablespoons snipped fresh chives
 ½ teaspoon chili powder
 ½ teaspoon salt
 ¼ teaspoon black pepper
     Chili powder (optional)

1. Preheat oven to 425°F. Grease well six 6-ounce ramekins or custard cups; place in a 13×9×2-inch baking pan. Set aside.
2. To roast peppers, halve peppers lengthwise; remove stems, seeds, and membranes. Place pepper halves, cut sides down, on a foil-lined baking sheet. Roast for 20 to 25 minutes or until peppers are charred and very tender. Wrap peppers in the foil. Let stand about 20 minutes or until cool enough to handle. Use a sharp knife to loosen edges of the skins; gently pull off the skins in strips and discard. Chop roasted peppers. Reduce oven temperature to 325°F.
3. In a large mixing bowl combine eggs and cream; stir in roasted peppers, corn kernels, cheese, bread crumbs, chives, chili powder, salt, and pepper. Stir gently until combined. Pour mixture evenly into the prepared ramekins. Place the baking pan on an oven rack. Pour boiling water into the pan around the ramekins to a depth of 1 inch.
4. Bake for 30 to 35 minutes or until a knife inserted near centers comes out clean. Remove ramekins from water. If desired, top each custard with additional chili powder. Serve warm.

PER SERVING *273 cal., 20 g fat (11 g sat. fat), 210 mg chol., 379 mg sodium, 14 g carb., 2 g fiber, 11 g pro.*

CHILE-CORN
CUSTARDS

PAELLA-STYLE
STUFFING

Paella-Style Stuffing

PREP 30 minutes
BAKE 25 minutes at 350°F
MAKES 6 servings

- 2 tablespoons canola oil
- ⅓ cup chopped onion (1 small)
- 3 cloves garlic, minced
- ⅔ cup short grain rice
- 1⅓ cups reduced-sodium chicken broth
- ¼ teaspoon saffron threads
- 6 ounces cooked smoked chorizo sausage, diced
- ¾ cup chopped red sweet pepper (1 medium)
- ½ cup thinly sliced celery (1 stalk)
- 2 tablespoons snipped fresh flat-leaf parsley
- ¼ teaspoon salt
- ¼ teaspoon black pepper
- 6 cups dried French bread cubes*
- ½ cup sliced pimiento-stuffed green olives
- 1¼ to 1½ cups reduced-sodium chicken broth
  Snipped fresh flat-leaf parsley (optional)

1. Preheat oven to 350°F. In a small saucepan heat 1 tablespoon of the oil over medium-high heat. Add onion; cook and stir about 3 minutes or until onion is tender. Add garlic; cook and stir for 30 seconds more. Add rice, stirring about 3 minutes or until rice just starts to brown. Carefully add the 1⅓ cups broth and the saffron threads. Bring to boiling; reduce heat. Cook, covered, about 15 minutes or until rice is cooked and liquid is absorbed.
2. Meanwhile, in a large skillet heat the remaining 1 tablespoon oil. Add chorizo, sweet pepper, and celery; cook and stir about 4 minutes or until chorizo begins to brown and vegetables are tender. Remove from heat. Add rice mixture, parsley, salt, and black pepper to mixture in skillet, tossing to combine.
3. In a large bowl combine rice mixture, bread cubes, and olives. Toss to mix. Drizzle with the 1¼ to 1½ cups broth to moisten, tossing to combine. Spoon stuffing into a buttered 2-quart baking dish or casserole. Cover with foil. Bake for 25 to 30 minutes or until heated through. If desired, sprinkle with additional snipped fresh parsley.

PER SERVING 408 cal., 19 g fat (5 g sat. fat), 240 mg chol., 1067 mg sodium, 43 g carb., 3 g fiber, 15 g pro.

*Tip For dry bread cubes, preheat oven to 300°F. Cut 8 ounces French bread into ¾-inch cubes (should yield 6 cups). Spread into a 15×10×1-inch baking pan. Bake for 10 to 15 minutes or until dry, stirring twice; cool. (Cubes will continue to dry and crisp as they cool.) Or let bread cubes stand, loosely covered, at room temperature for 8 to 12 hours.

Fondue Risotto

PREP 20 minutes COOK 4 minutes
SLOW COOK 1 hour 15 minutes
(high) STAND 15 minutes
MAKES 8 servings

- ⅔ cup sliced leeks (2 medium)
- 2 cloves garlic, minced
- 1 tablespoon butter
- 1¾ cups uncooked arborio rice
- 4 cups chicken broth
- ⅔ cup dry white wine
- ½ teaspoon cracked black pepper
- 2 ounces Gruyére or Swiss cheese, shredded
- 1 recipe Arugula Gremolata

1. In a large skillet cook and stir leeks and garlic in hot butter over medium heat for 3 to 5 minutes or until leeks are tender. Stir in rice; cook and stir for 1 minute more. Spoon rice mixture into a 3½- or 4-quart slow cooker. Stir in broth, wine, and pepper.
2. Cover and cook on high-heat setting for 1¼ hours or until rice is tender. Remove liner from cooker, if possible, or turn off cooker. Let risotto stand, uncovered, for 15 minutes before serving. Top with cheese and Arugula Gremolata.

Arugula Gremolata In a small bowl stir together 1 cup snipped arugula, 1 ounce crisp-cooked, drained and crumbled prosciutto, 2 tablespoons chopped toasted pine nuts (see tip, page 19), 1 tablespoon finely shredded lemon peel, and 1 clove minced garlic.

PER SERVING 224 cal., 6 g fat (3 g sat. fat), 18 mg chol., 553 mg sodium, 34 g carb., 1 g fiber, 7 g pro.

FONDUE RISOTTO

Peanut Butter and Chocolate Silk Pie

PREP 40 minutes BAKE 18 minutes at 425°F STAND 20 minutes CHILL 5 hours MAKES 10 servings

  1 recipe Chocolate Pastry
1½ cups whipping cream
  1 cup semisweet chocolate pieces
  ⅓ cup sugar
  ⅓ cup butter
  2 egg yolks, lightly beaten
  3 tablespoons crème de cacao or whipping cream
1½ cups whipping cream
  ⅓ cup creamy peanut butter
  ¼ cup sugar
  ¼ cup semisweet chocolate pieces, melted
  ½ cup chopped peanuts

1. Preheat oven to 425°F. Prepare Chocolate Pastry. On a lightly floured surface, use your hands to slightly flatten pastry. Roll pastry from center to edges into a circle about 12 inches in diameter. Wrap pastry around the rolling pin. Unroll into a 9-inch pie plate. Ease pastry into pie plate without stretching it. Trim pastry to ½ inch beyond edge of pie plate. Fold under pastry edge even with plate edge. Crimp edge as desired. Prick bottom and sides of pastry with a fork. Line pastry with a double thickness of foil. Bake for 10 minutes. Remove foil. Bake about 8 minutes more or until set and dry. Cool on a wire rack.

PEANUT BUTTER AND CHOCOLATE SILK PIE

2. For filling, in a medium-size heavy saucepan combine 1 cup of the whipping cream, the 1 cup chocolate pieces, ⅓ cup sugar, and butter. Stir over low heat about 10 minutes or until chocolate is melted. Remove from heat. Gradually stir half the hot mixture into egg yolks. Return egg yolk mixture to saucepan. Cook and stir over medium-low heat for 5 minutes or until slightly thickened and begins to bubble. Remove from heat. Stir in crème de cacao. Place saucepan in a bowl of ice water and let stand about 20 minutes or until mixture stiffens and becomes hard to stir, stirring occasionally.
3. Transfer chocolate mixture to a large mixing bowl. Beat with a mixer on medium to high for 2 to 3 minutes or until light and fluffy, scraping sides of bowl frequently. In a medium mixing bowl beat the remaining ½ cup whipping cream on medium until soft peaks form (tips curl). Fold some of the whipped cream into chocolate mixture to lighten. Fold chocolate mixture into the remaining whipped cream. Spread filling in pastry shell. Cover and chill for 5 to 24 hours.
4. For topping, before serving, in a large mixing bowl whisk together ¼ cup of the whipping cream, the peanut butter, and ¼ cup sugar until smooth. Gradually beat in the remaining 1¼ cups whipping cream on medium until soft peaks form (tips curl). Spread topping on pie. Drizzle with melted chocolate and sprinkle with peanuts.
Chocolate Pastry In a medium bowl stir together 1⅓ cups flour, 2 tablespoons sugar, 2 tablespoons cocoa powder, and ½ teaspoon salt. Using a pastry blender, cut in ½ cup shortening until mixture resembles coarse crumbs. Sprinkle 1 tablespoon ice water over part of the flour mixture; toss gently with a fork. Push moistened pastry to side of bowl. Repeat moistening pastry, using 1 tablespoon ice water at a time, until all the flour is moistened (3 to 4 tablespoons ice water total). Gather pastry into a ball, kneading gently until it holds together.
PER SERVING 733 cal., 59 g fat (29 g sat. fat), 152 mg chol., 243 mg sodium, 49 g carb., 3 g fiber, 10 g pro.

Almond-Clementine Lace Cookies

PREP 30 minutes
BAKE 7 minutes at 350°F
MAKES 20 servings

  ⅓ cup granulated sugar
  2 tablespoons butter, melted
  2 tablespoons light-color corn syrup
  1 teaspoon finely shredded clementine peel or orange peel
  1 tablespoon clementine juice or orange juice
  ½ cup finely chopped almonds
  ⅓ cup all-purpose flour
  1 cup whipping cream
  1 8-ounce carton sour cream
  ¾ cup powdered sugar
  1 teaspoon finely shredded clementine peel or orange peel
     Finely shredded clementine peel or orange peel (optional)

1. Preheat oven to 350°F. Line a cookie sheet with parchment paper; set aside.
2. In a small bowl combine granulated sugar, melted butter, corn syrup, 1 teaspoon clementine peel, and clementine juice. Stir in almonds and flour. Making only 3 or 4 cookies at a time, drop batter by rounded measuring teaspoons 3 inches apart onto the prepared cookie sheet. Bake for 7 to 8 minutes or until cookies are bubbly and deep golden brown.
3. Cool on cookie sheet for 1 to 2 minutes or just until set. Using a metal spatula, quickly remove cookies, one at a time and drape over a greased wooden spoon handle. When cookie is firm, slide it off the spoon handle and place it on a wire rack to cool. (If cookies harden before you shape them, reheat them in the 350°F oven about 1 minute or until softened.)
4. For filling, in a mixing bowl beat whipping cream, sour cream, powdered sugar, and 1 teaspoon clementine peel with a mixer on medium to high until soft peaks form (tips curl). Spoon filling into a decorating bag fitted with a large star tip. Pipe filling into cookies. If desired, sprinkle with additional clementine peel. Serve immediately.
PER SERVING 134 cal., 9 g fat (5 g sat. fat), 25 mg chol., 25 mg sodium, 13 g carb., 0 g fiber, 1 g pro.

**ALMOND-CLEMENTINE
LACE COOKIES**

Easy Weekend Food

WHEN HUNGRY HOUSEGUESTS arrive for the holidays, you need delicious, quick-to-fix food that fits into busy schedules. These recipes for casseroles, soups, and sandwiches are simple and satisfying —and easy on the cook.

CAJUN CHICKEN TARTS,
PAGE 150

Spinach, Butternut Squash, and Pasta Bake

PREP 35 minutes
ROAST 25 minutes at 425°F
BAKE 30 minutes at 350°F
MAKES 12 servings

- 1 3-pound butternut squash, peeled, seeded, and cut into ½-inch cubes
- 2 tablespoons olive oil
- 6 ounces dried cellentani pasta, or cavatappi or gemelli pasta
- 3 tablespoons butter
- ¾ cup finely chopped onion (1 large)
- 2 cloves garlic, minced
- 3 tablespoons all-purpose flour
- 2½ cups milk
- 2 cups shredded Fontina cheese (8 ounces)
- ½ cup grated Parmigiano-Reggiano cheese (2 ounce)
- 2 5-ounce packages fresh baby spinach, coarsely chopped
- 2 tablespoons finely snipped fresh sage
- ½ teaspoon salt
- ¼ teaspoon black pepper
- ¼ cup pine nuts

1. Preheat oven to 425°F. In a shallow roasting pan combine squash and olive oil; toss to coat. Roast about 25 minutes or until tender, stirring once. Remove squash from oven; reduce oven temperature to 350°F.
2. Meanwhile, cook pasta according to package directions; drain. Set aside. In a 6-quart Dutch oven melt butter over medium heat. Add onion and garlic; cook about 5 minutes or until onion is tender but not browned, stirring occasionally. Stir in flour; cook and stir for 1 minute. Add milk all at once. Cook and stir until thickened and bubbly. Stir in cheeses until melted. Stir in spinach until wilted. Stir in sage, salt, and pepper. Gently stir in cooked pasta and squash until combined. Transfer pasta mixture to a 3-quart baking dish. Cover with foil.
3. Bake for 20 minutes. Remove foil and top with pine nuts. Bake, uncovered, for 10 to 15 minutes more or until heated through.

PER SERVING 298 cal., 16 g fat (7 g sat. fat), 38 mg chol., 393 mg sodium, 29 g carb., 3 g fiber, 13 g pro.

Cajun Chicken Tarts

(photo page 148)

PREP 1 hour
BAKE 20 minutes at 425°F
MAKES 8 servings

- 1 recipe Cheese Pastry
- ⅓ cup butter
- ½ cup all-purpose flour
- 2 cups chopped onions (2 large)
- 1½ cups chopped red and/or green sweet peppers (2 medium)
- ¾ cup chopped celery
- 6 cloves garlic, minced
- 1 teaspoon Old Bay seasoning
- 2 14.5-ounce cans chicken broth
- 1 2- to 2½-pound purchased roasted chicken, shredded
- 8 ounces andouille sausage, chopped
- 8 ounces small fresh shrimp, peeled and deveined
- 1 egg, lightly beaten
- 1 tablespoon water
  Sliced green onions (optional)
  Old Bay seasoning (optional)

1. Prepare Cheese Pastry. Wrap pastry in plastic wrap until ready to use.
2. For sauce, in a 5- to 6-quart Dutch oven melt butter over medium heat. Stir in flour. Cook over medium heat for 10 to 12 minutes or until light reddish-brown (the color of a penny), stirring frequently. Add 2 cups onions, sweet peppers, and celery. Cook over medium-high heat for 3 minutes, stirring frequently. Add garlic and 1 teaspoon Old Bay seasoning; cook and stir for 1 minute more. Gradually stir in broth.
3. Bring gravy to boiling. Stir in chicken, sausage, and shrimp. Return to boiling; reduce heat. Simmer, uncovered, about 3 minutes or until shrimp are opaque.
4. Preheat oven to 425°F. Line two 15×10×1-inch baking pans with parchment paper; set aside. Using a slotted spoon, remove solid ingredients from sauce and place in a bowl. Cover gravy and keep warm, or reheat before serving.
5. Divide pastry into eight portions. On a lightly floured surface, roll each portion into an 8-inch circle; transfer to the prepared baking pans. Spoon about 1 cup of the chicken mixture onto each pastry circle to within 1 inch of the edges. Fold edges of pastry up and over filling, pleating as necessary. In a small bowl combine egg and the water; brush over pastry.
6. Bake for 20 to 25 minutes or until filling is heated through and pastry is golden, rearranging baking pans halfway through baking. If desired, sprinkle tarts with green onions and sprinkle reserved gravy with additional Old Bay seasoning. Serve tarts with gravy.
Cheese Pastry In a large bowl stir together 3 cups flour, ½ cup shredded sharp cheddar cheese, and 1 teaspoon salt. Using a pastry blender, cut in ¾ cup shortening until pieces are pea size. Sprinkle 1 tablespoon ice water

SPINACH, BUTTERNUT SQUASH, AND PASTA BAKE

over part of the flour mixture; toss gently with a fork. Push moistened pastry to side of bowl. Repeat moistening flour mixture, using 1 tablespoon ice water at a time, until all the pastry is moistened (9 to 12 tablespoons ice water total). Gather pastry into a ball, kneading gently until it holds together.

PER SERVING *734 cal., 43 g fat (15 g sat. fat), 189 mg chol., 1465 mg sodium, 49 g carb., 3 g fiber, 37 g pro.*

Kansas City Steak Soup

PREP 20 minutes COOK 25 minutes
MAKES 6 servings

- 1½ pounds lean ground beef
- 1 cup chopped onion (1 large)
- 1 cup sliced celery (2 stalks)
- 2 14.5-ounce cans 50% less sodium beef broth
- 1 28-ounce can diced tomatoes, undrained
- 1 10-ounce package frozen mixed vegetables
- 2 tablespoons steak sauce
- 2 teaspoons Worcestershire sauce
- ¼ teaspoon salt
- ¼ teaspoon black pepper
- ¼ cup all-purpose flour
  Snipped fresh flat-leaf parsley

1. In a large Dutch oven cook ground beef, onion, and celery over medium-high heat until meat is browned and vegetables are tender, using a wooden spoon to break up meat as it cooks. Drain off fat.
2. Stir in 1 can of the broth, the tomatoes, frozen vegetables, steak sauce, Worcestershire sauce, salt, and pepper. Bring to boiling; reduce heat. Simmer, covered, for 20 minutes.
3. In a medium bowl whisk together the remaining can of broth and flour; stir into soup in Dutch oven. Cook over medium-high heat until thickened and bubbly. Cook and stir for 1 minute more.
4. Ladle soup into bowls. Sprinkle each serving with parsley.

PER SERVING *306 cal., 12 g fat (5 g sat. fat), 74 mg chol., 747 mg sodium, 21 g carb., 4 g fiber, 27 g pro.*

KANSAS CITY STEAK SOUP

FRIED SMASHED
POTATOES

Fried Smashed Potatoes

PREP 20 minutes COOK 25 minutes
COOL 10 minutes
BAKE 22 minutes at 450°F
MAKES 12 servings

12 to 16 small red potatoes
    (1½ to 2 inches in diameter;
    1½ to 2 pounds total)
 1 teaspoon salt
 ¼ cup olive oil
 ¾ teaspoon salt
 ½ teaspoon black pepper
 ¾ cup freshly grated Parmesan
    cheese
 2 tablespoons finely chopped fresh
    flat-leaf parsley

1. Place potatoes in a large saucepan and
cover with at least 1 inch of water. Add
the 1 teaspoon salt to water. Bring to
boiling; reduce heat. Cover and simmer
for 25 to 30 minutes or until potatoes
are very tender; drain potatoes.
2. Preheat oven to 450°F. Transfer
potatoes to a foil-lined 15×10×1-inch
baking pan. Cool for 10 minutes. Using a
potato masher or the palm of your hand
(be careful not to burn your hand),
lightly press down on each potato
to smash to about ½-inch thickness,
keeping each potato in one piece.
3. Using half of the olive oil, brush
on potatoes. Sprinkle half of the
salt and pepper on potatoes. Bake,
uncovered, for 10 to 15 minutes or
until bottoms are lightly browned and
crisp. Turn potatoes; brush with the
remaining olive oil and sprinkle with
the remaining salt and pepper. Bake for
10 to 15 minutes more or until potatoes
are lightly browned and crisp. In a bowl
combine cheese and parsley. Sprinkle
on potatoes. Bake for 2 to 3 minutes
more or until cheese is melted.

PER SERVING *101 cal., 6 g fat*
(2 g sat. fat), 4 mg chol., 232 mg sodium,
9 g carb., 1 g fiber, 3 g pro.

PEPPER, OLIVE RELISH, AND SMOKED MOZZARELLA PANINI

Warm Sea Salt-and-Vinegar Green Bean Salad

START TO FINISH 25 minutes
MAKES 8 servings

- 1½ pounds green beans, trimmed
- 1 cup chopped red sweet pepper (1 large)
- ½ of a medium red onion, thinly sliced (1 cup)
- ⅓ cup white wine vinegar or champagne vinegar
- 2 teaspoons sugar
- 2 teaspoons Old Bay seafood seasoning
- 1½ teaspoons sea salt
- ¼ teaspoon cayenne pepper
- ¼ teaspoon cracked black pepper
- ¼ cup olive oil

1. In a Dutch oven cook green beans, covered, in a small amount of boiling lightly salted water about 8 minutes or just until crisp-tender, adding red sweet pepper and red onion to the water for the last 3 minutes of cooking; drain. Rinse with cold water; drain again.
2. Meanwhile, for vinaigrette, in a medium bowl whisk together vinegar, sugar, seafood seasoning, 1 teaspoon of the salt, the cayenne pepper, and black pepper. Whisk in oil.

3. Transfer green beans to a platter. Drizzle with vinaigrette; toss gently to coat. Sprinkle with the remaining ½ teaspoon salt before serving. Serve warm.
PER SERVING *105 cal., 7 g fat (1 g sat. fat), 0 mg chol., 387 mg sodium, 9 g carb., 3 g fiber, 2 g pro.*
To Make Ahead Prepare as directed. Cover and chill up to 24 hours. Serve chilled or at room temperature.

Pepper, Olive Relish, and Smoked Mozzarella Panini

START TO FINISH 40 minutes
MAKES 4 servings

- ½ cup finely chopped pitted green olives
- 2 tablespoons garlic-flavor oil or olive oil
- 2 teaspoons finely shredded lemon peel
  Salt and black pepper
- 1 large loaf Italian bread (about 18 inches long)
- 8 ounces sliced smoked or regular mozzarella cheese
- 4 bottled roasted red sweet peppers, drained
- 12 large fresh basil leaves
  Garlic-flavor oil or olive oil

  Pitted Kalamata olives (optional)
  Fresh spinach (optional)

1. For Olive Relish, in a small bowl combine green olives, the 2 tablespoons oil, and lemon peel. Season to taste with salt and black pepper.
2. Cut bread in half horizontally; cut crosswise into four portions. If desired, scoop out some of the insides from tops of bread. Place cheese slices on bottoms of bread. Layer with roasted peppers, Olive Relish, and basil. Replace tops one bread. Brush sandwiches with additional oil.
3. Preheat an electric sandwich press, a grill pan, or an extra-large skillet. Cover and cook sandwiches, half at a time, until bread is lightly toasted and cheese is melted. (If using a grill pan or skillet weight sandwiches with a heavy skillet. Cook until bread is lightly toasted. Turn sandwiches, weight, and cook until bread is lightly toasted and cheese is melted.)
4. If desired, top each sandwich with a wooden pick threaded with a Kalamata olive and spinach leaf.
PER SERVING *600 cal., 29 g fat (12 g sat. fat), 60 mg chol., 1441 mg sodium, 65 g carb., 5 g fiber, 22 g pro.*

Chocolate Shortbread Blondies with Macaroon Topping

PREP 25 minutes
BAKE 40 minutes at 350°F
MAKES 32 servings

3½ cups all-purpose flour
⅔ cup granulated sugar
½ cup unsweetened cocoa powder
1⅔ cups butter
½ cup miniature semisweet chocolate pieces
1 recipe Macaroon Topping
2 cups packed brown sugar
2 eggs
2 teaspoons vanilla
1 teaspoon baking powder
¼ teaspoon baking soda
1 cup chopped salted cashews or peanuts
   Milk chocolate, melted (optional)

1. Preheat oven to 350°F. Line a 13×9×2-inch baking pan with foil, extending the foil over edges of pan. Grease foil; set pan aside. For crust, in a medium bowl stir together 1½ cups of the flour, the granulated sugar, and cocoa powder. Using a pastry blender, cut in 1 cup of the butter until mixture resembles coarse crumbs. Stir in chocolate pieces. Press dough evenly onto the bottom of the prepared baking pan. Bake for 8 minutes or until set. Prepare Macaroon Topping; set aside.
2. Meanwhile, in a medium saucepan stir brown sugar and the remaining ⅔ cup butter over medium heat until melted and smooth; cool slightly. Add eggs, one at a time, beating with a wooden spoon after each addition just until combined. Stir in vanilla. Stir in the remaining 2 cups flour, baking powder, and baking soda. Stir in cashews.
3. Pour batter evenly over crust. Spoon Macaroon Topping in small mounds on top of batter; carefully spread to edges of pan. Bake for 32 to 34 minutes or until topping is lightly browned. Cool in pan on a wire rack.
4. If desired, drizzle with melted milk chocolate. Using the edges of the foil, lift uncut bars out of pan. Cut into 32 bars.
Macaroon Topping In a medium bowl stir together ⅓ cup granulated sugar and ¼ cup all-purpose flour. Stir in 1¼ cups sweetened flaked coconut, 3 lightly beaten egg whites, and ½ teaspoon vanilla.
PER SERVING *291 cal., 15 g fat (9 g sat. fat), 37 mg chol., 160 mg sodium, 38 g carb., 1 g fiber, 4 g pro.*

Autumn Maple-Pear Pie

PREP 1 hour
BAKE 1 hour 10 minutes at 375°F
MAKES 8 servings

1 recipe Nut Pastry
3 tablespoons packed brown sugar
2 tablespoons all-purpose flour
1 teaspoon apple pie spice
6 cups peeled (if desired) and thinly sliced pears (6 medium)
½ cup maple syrup
1 egg, lightly beaten
1 tablespoon water
   Poached Pear Slices (optional)*
   Caramel-flavor ice cream topping (optional)

1. Preheat oven to 375°F. Prepare Nut Pastry. On a lightly floured surface, slightly flatten one pastry ball. Roll pastry from center to edges into a circle about 12 inches in diameter. Wrap pastry around the rolling pin. Unroll pastry into a 9-inch pie plate; ease into pie plate without stretching it.
2. For filling, in a large bowl stir together brown sugar, flour, and apple pie spice. Add 6 cups pears; toss gently to coat. Transfer filling to pastry-lined pie plate. Drizzle with maple syrup. Trim pastry even with pie plate rim. Roll the remaining pastry ball into a 12-inch-diameter circle. Place pastry on filling; trim to ½ inch beyond edge of pie plate. Fold top pastry edge under bottom pastry. Crimp as desired.
3. Using a sharp knife, cut several large slits in top pastry. In a small bowl combine egg and the water. Brush pastry with egg mixture.
4. Tent pie with foil. Bake for 45 minutes. Remove foil. Bake for 25 to 30 minutes more or until pears are tender and filling is bubbly. Cool on a wire rack.
5. Meanwhile, if desired, prepare Poached Pear Slices. Before serving, place the poached pear slice with the stem in center of pie and drizzle with caramel topping. Top individual servings with remaining pear slices and drizzle with caramel topping.
Nut Pastry In bowl combine 2¼ cups flour; ¼ cup ground, toasted pecans (see tip, page 19); and 1 teaspoon salt. Cut in ½ cup shortening and butter until pieces are pea size. Sprinkle 1 tablespoon cold water over part of mixture; toss with fork. Push moistened dough to side. Using a total of 8 to 12 tablespoons, repeat until all the dough is moistened. Divide in half; form each into a ball.
PER SERVING *468 cal., 21 g fat (7 g sat. fat), 39 mg chol., 357 mg sodium, 66 g carb., 5 g fiber, 6 g pro.*
*Poached Pear Slices In a medium saucepan combine 1 cup sugar, 1 cup water, 1 tablespoon lemon juice, and 2 inches stick cinnamon. Bring to boiling, stirring until sugar is dissolved. Cut a large pear from top to bottom into ¼-inch slices (include the stem with one of the slices); remove seeds. Add pear slices to sugar mixture. Return to boiling; reduce heat. Simmer, uncovered, for 5 minutes or just until tender. Using a slotted spoon, transfer pear slices to a wire rack set in a shallow baking pan. Cool pear slices; discard syrup.

CHOCOLATE SHORTBREAD BLONDIES WITH MACAROON TOPPING

AUTUMN MAPLE-
PEAR PIE